Getting Your
to Behave

Getting Your Class to Behave

Sixth Edition

Sue Cowley

BLOOMSBURY EDUCATION

LONDON OXFORD NEW YORK NEW DELHI SYDNEY

BLOOMSBURY EDUCATION
Bloomsbury Publishing Plc
50 Bedford Square, London, WC1B 3DP, UK
29 Earlsfort Terrace, Dublin 2, Ireland

BLOOMSBURY, BLOOMSBURY EDUCATION and the Diana logo are trademarks of
Bloomsbury Publishing Plc

First published in Great Britain 2001 as *Getting the Buggers to Behave* by
Continuum International Publishing Group

This edition published in Great Britain 2024 by Bloomsbury Publishing Plc
Text copyright © Sue Cowley Books Ltd 2024

A catalogue record for this book is available from the British Library.

ISBN: PB: 978-1-8019-9432-3; ePub: 978-1-8019-9429-3; ePDF: 978-1-8019-9431-6

2 4 6 8 10 9 7 5 3 1

Typeset by Newgen KnowledgeWorks Pvt. Ltd., Chennai, India
Printed and bound in India by Replika Press Pvt. Ltd

To find out more about our authors and books visit www.bloomsbury.com
and sign up for our newsletters

Contents

Acknowledgements

Many thanks go to all the teachers, practitioners, support staff, children and young people who I've worked with over the years. Your inspiration, ideas, advice and support are the framework on which this book was written and updated. Teaching often seems to run in the family, so I must also thank my mum and my aunt for inspiring me to go into the profession.

Thanks to all the team at Bloomsbury, especially my Editor, Joanna Ramsay. And as always, very special thanks and love to Tilak, Álvie and Rui.

Author's note

It's been more than two decades now since I first sat down in a small back bedroom in Somerset and wrote this book. I can still remember vividly how the words spilled out of me and onto the page. In a sense, it was a book that wrote itself: a distillation of all I'd experienced in the first part of my teaching career. At that point, I'd got through the newly qualified bit, taught in primary and secondary schools, worked overseas, done supply teaching, taken on a promoted post, taught in schools where handling behaviour was (in that classic euphemism), a 'challenge'. I had found useful strategies for dealing with inappropriate behaviour, and I wanted to share them with the world.

In the time that's gone by since then, I've been fortunate enough to work, train and talk with hundreds of thousands of people in education, all around the world: early career and experienced teachers, teaching assistants, support staff, early years practitioners, librarians, further education tutors, university lecturers, senior leaders, trainee teachers, prison educators, peripatetic specialist teachers, and countless others who help children, young people and adults to learn. I've also had a couple of kids of my own, so I've seen education through the eyes of a parent as well. Through these experiences, I've picked up lots more ideas about encouraging positive behaviours and gained insights into what works in the full range of contexts. The basic tenets of this book remain faithful to the original, but I've adapted, developed and improved it.

If you've read previous editions of this book, you might notice that I've changed the title for this version. I've been joking with friends and family that I have 'cancelled myself'. On a more serious note, though, language matters and (especially in the current climate), I need to listen to the people who have said they are uncomfortable with the title's wording. Originally intended as a jokey allusion to what exasperated teachers might say in the privacy of the staffroom, this book's original title has had its day. And so, my aim with this new edition is to give you lots of practical strategies and techniques for *getting **your class** to behave!*

Introduction

With a class who behave well, teaching is one of the most wonderful jobs in the world. Every day offers you a new and different experience: the chance to see children discover fresh concepts, to learn something they never knew before, and the opportunity to make a real difference to their lives. Unfortunately, with a poorly behaved class, it becomes much harder to enjoy your job. You are in the classroom to teach, but unless you can get behaviour sorted first, it's very hard to fulfil that role. One of the most essential characteristics of an effective teacher is the ability to handle the behaviour of a class, so that the learners can get on with learning. This book is designed to help you do that, by offering you a wealth of practical ideas to try out in your setting.

Teachers use a wide range of skills in their daily work: you need to be a specialist at teaching your subjects, you must be a skilled communicator, and you need to manage your class's behaviour. At its heart, behaviour management is about relationships – building them, sustaining them, constantly working on them. To an extent, you learn to do this through being in the classroom. As time goes on, and you gain in experience, you find yourself drawing from a bank of ideas and strategies. There are some teachers who are naturally good at regulating the behaviour of others; who have an innate ability to engage with and 'hold' their class. But it's also possible to improve and increase your behaviour management skills, whatever your starting point, and that is exactly what my book should help you do.

This book is practical, down-to-earth and easy to read. No academic theory – just lots of tips, advice and examples to show how the ideas I give work in practice. Although I address my suggestions mainly to teachers, you might also find this book helpful if you work in any role within education (as a classroom assistant, school librarian, lunchtime supervisor, peripatetic music teacher, play-worker, and so on). The ideas and advice given here are based on common-sense observations and strategies that have worked for me and the teachers I have met. There is no 'magic solution', no 'silver bullet' waiting for you in these pages – just honest and realistic advice. My hope is that you find this book a useful reference – one that you can turn to for ideas whenever you need them, or to find alternative strategies for managing your class.

Teachers today are stressed – by the workload, the paperwork, the accountability system and, of course, behaviour. What I aim to give you in this book are ways of minimising the stress, which is why it focuses mainly on strategies for *you*, rather than for your learners. What I'm interested in doing is helping you survive day to day in a challenging job, and allowing you to enjoy the amazing career you have chosen. I do hope that this book helps you in getting your class to behave. Because, if you can get it right, not only will you improve the chances for each of your learners, but you'll also be able to thrive and flourish in the wonderful career that you've chosen.

Please note: to simplify things, in this book I use the word 'learners' to apply to whoever it is you're teaching. To you they might be children, pupils, teenagers, students, young people, adults: 'learner' was the most all-encompassing term I could find.

You can follow Sue Cowley on Twitter @Sue_Cowley and join the conversation using #GYCTB.

Part One

In the Beginning

Chapter 1

Key Principles of Positive Behaviour Management

What are the key principles?

In this first chapter, I take a look at the key principles: the fundamental ground rules of managing and supporting your learners' behaviour. These techniques need to become intuitive if you hope to get consistently appropriate behaviour. Indeed, this is why experienced teachers sometimes seem to have a 'magic' touch with their classes. They are using the key principles instinctively: the strategies have become a subconscious part of their teaching. That is not to say that doing these things will automatically *guarantee* you appropriate behaviour, but you stand a much better chance of getting that once they are in place.

The key principles are:

- **Be definite**: *'I'm clear about the behaviours we need for learning.'*
- **Be aware**: *'I know what my options are for responding to behaviour.'*
- **Be calm and consistent**: *'I'm always polite and fair to you.'*
- **Give them structure**: *'I know where we're going.'*
- **Be positive**: *'You're doing great!'*
- **Be interested**: *'You're people as well as learners.'*
- **Be flexible**: *'I know when to bend rather than break.'*
- **Be persistent**: *'I refuse to give up.'*
- **Engage them**: *'I want you to want to learn.'*

If you're new to the profession, the key principles will give you a great foundation for the journey you're about to take. They're essentially a set of common-sense ideas about managing behaviour and building good relationships. If you've been working in education for a while, and you're experiencing issues with behaviour, take a look at the key principles to see whether there is something relatively simple that you can tweak.

Be definite

'I'm clear about the behaviours we need for learning.'

The first (and most important) of the key principles is to come across to your learners as being someone who knows what they want and need in terms of behaviour. There are three parts to this. You've got to:

1 Know what you expect from your learners.

2 Communicate this to them so there are no ambiguities.

3 Create the perception that you are confident about getting what you've asked for.

If you think about it, it's only fair to have clarity of expectations. You can't claim that your learners are 'misbehaving' unless you've made it clear what 'behaving' looks like in the first place. Let's take a look at the three aspects in turn.

1 Know what you expect from your learners

This is harder than it sounds, especially when you first start out in teaching. There will be lots of things you want, but which are your priorities, and how do you get this information across? In theory, the behaviour policy at your school or setting should outline the rules. Certainly, there will be some 'absolutes' – whole-school edicts on mobile phones, chewing gum, swearing, and so on. But although this gives you a starting point, in reality you must establish your own set of standards and work out what your own expectations are. This will partly depend on your teaching style (see Chapter 5 'Teaching Styles'). If you're working in a very challenging school environment, you'll have to figure out your priorities: what really matters, and what can wait until you've established a working relationship with the young people? If you're a secondary teacher dealing with learners in different year groups, you might have slightly different expectations of your youngest learners and your oldest ones. It can take a good couple of years to get this all worked out in your mind and to figure out how you are going to run your classroom.

It's probably helpful at this point if I give you my own top three expectations of how a group should behave. These apply equally if I'm working with children, teenagers or adults, although the way that I express them will differ.

- *We use one voice* – we listen silently when anyone is addressing the whole group, so that learning can take place. This applies when the teacher is speaking and also when the other learners are too.

- *We show each other respect* – we treat others as we would expect them to treat us.

- *We always give it a go* – we try our hardest and do our best.

And, of course, the teacher must try their very hardest to fulfil these expectations as well.

It pays to be very specific about everything that learners do in your lessons. If you don't give exact details of what you want, they will have to work it out for themselves by pushing at the boundaries until you say 'stop!' It is far better to be clear from the word go.

However, don't introduce too many expectations right at the start, as too much information will just confuse your class, and they won't be able to retain it all. Instead, drip-feed your expectations in as required. For instance, the first time you do group work, talk about how this should be done; the first time you line up the class, discuss how they should do this, and so on.

2 Communicate it to them so there are no ambiguities

Once you know exactly what you want, you've got to get it across to your class, using clear, simple and age-appropriate language. One useful way to do this is to use 'I expect', 'I want' or 'we need' statements, depending on the kind of teaching style you wish to communicate.

'I expect' might come across as more adult-led, whereas 'we need' is a more about a sense of community. It can work very well to phrase your expectations using 'we' ('we always listen'), to give a sense of the whole group working together.

Some teachers like to work out their expectations together with the children, particularly in primary schools, where you are teaching one class for the entire year. Primary teachers will often create a 'class charter' or whole-class agreement about behaviour, which the children might sign. This can work really well, as it creates a sense of partnership and team work. However, it can be tricky for new teachers to manage, as it can come across as the teacher being a bit unsure of what they want. Typically, you will end up getting the learners to come up with the rules that you wanted in the first place. It is worth considering whether it would be quicker and simpler just to tell them, especially if you are new to teaching and you need to project an air of confidence.

3 Create the perception that you are confident about getting what you've asked for

Like predators sensing a weakness in their prey, young people are instinctively aware of uncertainty in their teachers. (Think back to when you were at school – I bet there were some teachers you knew you could push around, and others you knew you couldn't!) A key part of achieving your expectations is to communicate an air of confidence to your class. Some people are able to do this naturally; others find it a real struggle and it takes them a few years to get this sorted. It has a lot to do with how well you use verbal and non-verbal communication. In short, some of the strategies you're after include:

- lots of eye contact
- a clear and engaging tone of voice
- plenty of movement around the space
- open and relaxed body language
- a refusal to overreact, or to become defensive.

I cover all these approaches in more detail later on in this book, particularly in Chapters 4 and 5.

Of course, there will be situations where, despite your best efforts, some, many or most of the learners refuse to comply with your expectations. At these times, it is very tempting to give up, to say '*whatever*' and let the learners behave as they wish. But maintaining high standards and refusing to give up on your expectations is, in the long run, the key to success. It tells your learners that you believe they are capable of great things, and that you won't allow them to let themselves down.

When you first start out in teaching, you may feel inclined to play the role of friend rather than authority figure. It can feel unfair to make demands of your learners. But actually, you're doing them a favour by giving them clear boundaries. Young people want certainty from the adults in their lives. They need you to create and enforce boundaries to give them a feeling of security. They want you to create a calm and well- ordered environment for learning. This is particularly important for the learners who give you most difficulty in terms of their behaviour, because they may lack structure outside of school.

Be aware

'*I know what my options are for responding to behaviour.*'

The second of my basics deals with what happens when your learners are, or are not, meeting your expectations. Hopefully, at least some of the time, most of your class will be doing as you've asked. When this happens, don't just breathe a silent sigh of relief and stay quiet in the hope that it continues. Acknowledge their appropriate behaviour – note and reward it to encourage them to behave in this way again. One of the simplest and most valuable rewards of all, particularly where the class respects the teacher, is to give them specific, detailed praise. ('That's brilliant, Year 6; every single one of you is listening really well today. I'm absolutely delighted with you!')

Some of the time, however, you will have at least a few learners who are *not* doing what you want. The way you react when this happens has a powerful influence on your overall chances of behaviour success. When you face low-level inappropriate behaviour, you have three basic options:

1 **The instinctive reaction:** The teacher gets cross and turns straight to consequences – this is the reaction you have to fight. Far better to stay calm and deal with the problem using low-level strategies.

2 **The rational reaction:** The teacher looks around for what's going right and before doing anything else, highlights some examples of appropriate behaviour ('That's great, Joe, you're waiting silently for the lesson to begin. You obviously want to go to break on time.').

3 **The creative reaction:** The teacher thinks, 'How can I deal with this differently?' and uses a non-verbal signal, a distraction, a change of pace or an interesting motivator to encourage the learners back on track.

There will be occasions when consequences are necessary – when the inappropriate behaviour justifies an instant negative response. In these circumstances, you must understand the options available to you. You and your learners must be certain about this: behaviour 'X' leads to consequence 'Y', every time it happens. You need your learners to understand the connection between their current behaviour and the consequence they will receive if it continues. This puts the decision in their hands: if they understand the rules and the consequences, it is in their power to make a good choice, although it's important to bear in mind that children who have yet to fully develop their self-regulation skills will find this more difficult than others.

The consequence you use depends on the policy of the school or setting where you work, and on the age of the learner involved, for instance:

- **Early years:** a disappointed look, a short period of 'thinking time', talking things over together with the learner.
- **Primary:** missing free choice or 'golden time', a chat with parents or carers at home time.
- **Secondary:** a break-time detention, being put 'on report'.
- **Further education:** being given a 'disciplinary' warning.

When a learner challenges your expectations, try the following:

- Be *definite* about what you want, and stick to it.
- Praise those who are doing what you asked, to model what you're looking for.
- Stay calm, cool and polite throughout the encounter.
- Clarify any potential misunderstandings – ask if support is needed.
- State what you need the learner to do – frame it positively.

- State what will happen if the learner refuses to do as you ask and makes a poor choice.
- Don't get distracted from your original point.
- Don't get drawn into a discussion or a debate.
- Depersonalise the situation – it's about the behaviour, not the person.
- Sound sad or disappointed about having to give a consequence.
- If necessary, apply the consequence.
- If appropriate, offer a 'way out'.

As well as thinking about the kinds of rewards and consequences that you might use to react to inappropriate behaviour, it is also helpful to consider what the behaviours you see might be 'telling' you and what options you might have in response to that information. The younger your learners are, the more likely it is that their behaviours will be trying to communicate something to you – whether that's about not understanding what's going on, needing a change of direction to retain their focus, or a symptom of some additional needs.

Thinking about behaviour as a form of communication does not mean attending to everything that your learners try to communicate to you. It simply means reflecting on your own approach, to see if there is anything you could tweak or change to support behaviour better. It's about considering all the possibilities beyond just 'they're refusing to behave', rather than making assumptions. For instance:

- Children squirming on the carpet might be communicating that they have reached the limit of their concentration and need to get up and move.
- Learners struggling to get started on a task might be communicating they don't understand the explanation and need you to go through it again.
- A young person repeatedly playing 'class clown' might be trying to hide their struggles with literacy.

Here's an example of a teacher dealing with inappropriate behaviour, to show you how 'being aware' might work. This is based on a typical lower-secondary school scenario: a learner refusing to do as they are asked. Throughout the book you'll find lots of examples based on other age groups.

For example...

Ella arrives at the drama studio and walks in without taking her shoes off. The teacher has set a rule that learners take off their shoes before entering the room.

Teacher: Ella, please go back outside and take off your shoes. [*The teacher states the expectation clearly.*]

Ella: I can't.

Teacher: Come on, Ella, you know the rule in drama that we take off our shoes. Look, everyone's ready, let's get on with the lesson. [*The teacher restates her expectation, rather than asking why Ella can't take off her shoes.*]

Ella: But I've sprained my ankle. I can't take them off.

Teacher: Do you have a note about your ankle? [*The teacher checks for veracity – is there a genuine issue here – but refuses to be distracted.*]

Ella: No.

Teacher: Then I need you to go back outside and take off your shoes, thanks Ella. [*The teacher restates the original request, reinforcing it by saying 'thanks'.*]

Ella: No. I won't. Are you gonna make me?

Teacher: Oh Ella, if you won't take off your shoes, I will have to pass a red slip to your head of year. Don't make me do that. [*The teacher refuses to get riled, but has had enough of this.*]

Ella: That's not fair.

Teacher: Last chance [*pulls out red slip*], three… two… one. [*Ella grudgingly takes off her shoes.*]

Just to show how differently this encounter *might* have turned out, let's re-run the scene…

Teacher: Ella, go back outside and take off your shoes.

Ella: I can't.

Teacher: What do you mean, 'I can't'? Of course you can. [*The teacher asks a pointless rhetorical question.*]

Ella: But I've sprained my ankle. I really can't take them off.

Teacher: Don't be so stupid. Just get on with it. [*The teacher is dismissive and rude, rather than checking if this is true.*]

Ella: Don't call me stupid.

Teacher: Look, just go outside and take off your shoes. Now! [*The teacher is starting to get really cross.*]

Ella: No. I won't. You gonna make me?

Teacher: Right, that's it. Go to the head of year. Get out of my sight! [*Ella stomps off, swearing under her breath.*]

Be calm and consistent

'I'm always polite and fair to you.'

We all welcome calmness and consistency: we like to know what to expect from the people in our lives, and it throws us if we get an unpredictable response. For some children who struggle to behave, this is the problem they face at home – they never know what the reaction to their behaviour will be. Our duty as professionals is to provide our learners with a calm, consistent and considered model of adult behaviour and responses.

It's not easy to be fair and polite all the time – staying calm in the face of inappropriate behaviour is hard. This is because of the fight-or-flight response. The learner or class 'attacks' you by not listening. You experience a rush of adrenaline and feel the urge to attack back. Alternatively, you want to run away from the situation. Neither of these options is available to us – we can't lash out, and we can't leave.

Although it's difficult, the hard truth is that, if you can remain tirelessly calm and consistent at all times, there is far less chance of confrontation arising. You also avoid creating unnecessary stress for yourself. An excellent rule of thumb is to treat your learners as you would treat another adult (for instance, if you worked in an office), no matter how difficult their behaviour is.

To help yourself stay calm, it can help to have your own techniques and methods to short-circuit that fight-or-flight response. You could:

- Take a few deep breaths.
- Count to ten.
- Look out of the window to remind yourself that there is a world beyond your classroom.

As well as staying calm, you've also got to be consistent: the standard should stay the same, wherever the inappropriate behaviour happens and whoever it involves. This is much harder to do than it might sound. Sometimes you will be tired, stressed, in a hurry and under pressure to get on with the lesson. Some learners will 'get on your nerves' and your subconscious reactions to prior difficult encounters can affect the approach you take with them.

Learners are extremely sensitive to the idea of fairness. Some will feel that they are unfairly singled out and that, once they have behaved poorly, they get picked on over and over again. If we are honest, it's natural that we like some learners more than others. However, our personal feelings should not come into it – we must treat all learners in an equitable way, despite any personal preferences we might feel. Find something to 'like' in every child, especially those who have a difficult life outside of school.

Consistency is a 'holy grail' for headteachers and senior managers, and with good reason. Where members of staff apply the rules and consequences in a completely consistent way, the learners are presented with a single set of standards. But if behaviour 'X' is okay with one person and not with another, then the learners get confused about where the boundaries lie. You can support your fellow staff by being as consistent as you possibly can be.

Remember, consistency is not the same as inflexibility. It's the *standard* that needs to remain consistent, rather than the approach. Some learners will need gentle coaxing and reasonable adjustments to reach the standards that others attain with ease. Just like you adapt your teaching to support the needs of everyone in your class, so you can incorporate flexible ways of communicating around behaviour.

Give them structure

'I know where we're going.'

Our natural impulse is to place a structure on our lives – a daily pattern that gives us a feeling of safety and security. For the learners who give us most difficulty in our classrooms and teaching spaces, this structure is probably missing from their worlds. At home, their parents or carers may not have set boundaries for them, or they may constantly move the goalposts, reacting in a variety of different ways to the same types of inappropriate behaviour. Their homes lives may be chaotic, unstructured, unsafe. School can offer a refuge for these young people, a place where they meet adults who give them suitable and consistent guidelines about what appropriate behaviour actually looks like.

There are lots of ways you can offer structure to your learners: through clear lesson content, through classroom organisation, through the methods you use to control behaviour. Once you have a clear structure in your own mind, this clarity will be apparent to your class, and it will help you to stay calm and feel confident. Make it clear to your learners at every stage exactly how and why certain structures are being used, making them explicit and as clear as possible. For instance, talking at the start of the lesson about the sequence of the learning, using 'first, next, then, finally'.

When you achieve a sense of purpose, clarity and structure, this has many ongoing benefits which build on one another:

Here are some areas of your teaching you can structure, and examples of the routines you might use with different age groups:

- **Start of day/lesson:** circle time, register, lining up outside the room, starter activity.
- **Use of space:** carpet time, groupings, layout of desks, seating plans.

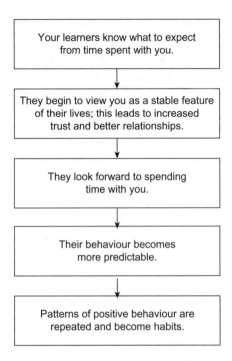

- **The learning:** use of objectives, success criteria, plenary at the end of lesson time.
- **The resources:** how these are collected, where they are stored, use of volunteers to hand them out as a motivator.
- **Expected learning behaviours:** learners working quietly, staying in seats, hands up to give an answer, use of talk partners.
- **End of sessions:** homework set, learners stand behind chairs, leaving one by one, story time, playing a short game.

Be positive

'You're doing great!'

'Stress the positive' is, or should be, a mantra for teachers. The whole area of motivation is a tricky one, and I deal with this in greater detail in Chapter 6. It can sometimes feel as though we are praising our learners for just about anything to try to get them on our side. But this is a mistake: if we set our sights low, then this low level is where our learners will aim. If we have high standards, and expect great things, children and young people learn to strive for their best. Being positive is not just about praising your learners, it's also about having a positive outlook during your time with them. The discriminating use of praise, and the ability to remain relentlessly positive, will help you a great deal in managing behaviour. It should also make you less susceptible to stress and negative emotions in your daily working life.

Here are a few of my top tips for staying positive with your learners:

- Greet your class with a positive expectation – 'Great to see you; we're going to do some really good learning today.'
- Expect the best from your class, rather than anticipating the worst.
- Focus on the learners who are doing the right thing and highlight this, even if it feels a bit 'fake'.
- Frame what you say in a positive light – use 'do' rather than 'don't'.
- Avoid accusing your learners or criticising them.
- Tread very carefully with sarcasm and avoid it completely with younger children.
- React to inappropriate behaviour by suggesting a positive alternative.
- Use praise of individuals to encourage the whole group.
- Use rewards in preference to consequences as far as possible (a useful ratio is about five to one).
- Set targets to give positive ways for learners to improve.
- See completion of targets as a chance to use praise or to give a reward.

Here are two examples of the same situation – a teacher inviting a class into the room – to show the difference between a positive and a negative approach.

For example...

Negative

'Come on, hurry up! Why are you being so slow? Come on, come on, we've got loads to get through today and we'll never get everything done if you're this slow. What's wrong with you? Why are you making so much noise?'

I know how I'd feel about being in this teacher's class – unfairly accused and inclined to behave poorly. Immediately, the learners are criticised for being slow. The teacher creates a negative feeling about the learning they will be doing, putting the blame on the learners for not being able to get through it all. Finally, they use two negative questions to suggest that the learners are always this bad. By starting the lesson in such a negative frame of mind, the teacher's expectations may well be met.

Positive

'Right, if you can all come in as quickly as possible, I've got some exciting things for you to do today. We need to get started straight away, so that we can get through them all. That's an excellent level of noise. Well done. Now let's see if you can be even quieter.'

Here, the teacher tells the learners how they should come into the room. They create a sense of purpose and interest, by telling the learners that they have some 'really exciting' things planned for them. Finally, the teacher praises them for the low level of noise, but sets them the challenge of being even quieter. By starting the lesson in this way, a positive atmosphere should be created and sustained.

Be interested

'You're people as well as learners.'

At its heart, effective behaviour management is about positive teacher/learner relationships. After all, you hopefully came into teaching at least partly because you love working with children, young people, or just learners in general. If your learners respect you, and feel that you respect them, this will inevitably lead to better behaviour. A key part of building respect is to take an interest in what makes your learners tick – to care about what makes them remarkable as individual people, as well as them just being learners passing through your bit of the education system.

Taking an interest in your learners is particularly helpful when you are experiencing behaviour problems. If a whole class is messing you around because they find a topic or subject boring, then you might be able to incorporate some elements of their latest interest into the learning. It might be superheroes, dinosaurs, *Peppa Pig*, Minecraft, Fortnite or the latest music star – whatever 'floats their boat' as the saying goes. If an individual learner is behaving poorly, take an interest in what motivates them: this may help you to devise a suitable reward system.

To make better connections with your learners, try:

- asking them about their interests
- referring to shared interests in class

- getting involved in extracurricular activities
- making a point of saying 'hello' when you see them outside of lessons
- keeping up to date with the latest trends
- being open to their ideas, and interested in their opinions.

Be flexible

'I know when to bend rather than break.'

There are times as a teacher when you need to learn how to bend a little, for your learners' sake and also for your own. Achieving a balance between this flexibility, and the certainty, clarity and consistency already discussed, is one of the hardest and most subtle of all teaching skills. Sometimes, and only sometimes, you will need to relax your boundaries and accept that you are not going to achieve everything that you had initially hoped. By giving a little leeway when it is appropriate, your learners will develop greater respect for you as a person and as a teacher.

A flexible approach means you tend to find more inventive and interesting ways around problems. Rather than coming at an issue head on and refusing to budge or adapt, be willing to take a lateral approach if that is going to work better. It's about being flexible in your thinking and in your teaching to help you manage behaviour. For instance, imagine you have a Year 2 class who are always tricky last thing on a Thursday afternoon in the summer term, partly because they get tired, and also because by that stage in the week the room is really hot and stuffy. You might battle on regardless, getting into arguments and damaging the good relationship you normally have with them. Alternatively, you might apply a bit of flexibility and take them into the hall or playground for this time, doing practical rather than written work.

Flexibility is very much a matter of personal taste and individual circumstances – it is about knowing when it is appropriate to compromise. In some situations, learners respond very well to a teacher who bends a little on occasions; in other settings, the learners see any flexibility as a cue to start pushing at the boundaries. In some very challenging schools, where inappropriate behaviour is a complex and deep-rooted issue, taking a 'zero tolerance' approach could mean being left with only a handful of learners to actually teach. Trust your judgement on this – don't see it as a personal failure if you have to bend more than you might wish to stay afloat.

There are various situations in which you might offer flexibility to your learners:

- **With the class:** if your class is never in the mood for work on Friday afternoons, you will achieve very little if you cannot learn to be flexible. Accept that this situation is outside your control. Aim to achieve a reasonable amount of work, negotiating targets and talking about how fair you are being.

Many primary teachers set this time up as a reward, using a period of 'golden time' last lesson of the week to help them manage behaviour in other lessons.

- **With the work:** on occasions, when your class has a good reason not to be in the mood to work, you might like to offer a compromise. If the learners can complete a specified part of the activity, you could allow them to chat quietly for a few minutes at the end of the lesson as a reward. With older learners, you could frame this time as their 'golden time' (a 'chill time' if you like). This could be time that they must earn with appropriate behaviour, or that they could lose if they don't get the work done.

- **With the individual:** some learners simply do not want to be in education; school seems entirely irrelevant to their lives. In these situations, find a balance – set small and achievable targets, but don't torment yourself if a learner decides to opt out. Where a very troubled young person is always confrontational with you, particularly when you use consequences, try backing off for a while to give yourselves both a break.

In teaching, there's a tricky balance to be struck between consistency and the flexibility that is essential for day-to-day survival. A good way to think about this is that you have to differentiate your approaches to behaviour, just as you would differentiate the activities you set for learning. This doesn't mean adapting or dropping your standards; it means you go about achieving those standards in a variety of ways, depending on the individual needs of the learner. With a quiet, cooperative young person, a quick word might be enough to get uniform sorted. With a child whose behaviour is very challenging, a quiet, calm whispered request when the class is settled on a task might work best.

Be persistent

'I refuse to give up.'

The ideas and approaches in this book are not a magic panacea – a formula that guarantees instant success: there is no such thing when it comes to handling behaviour. Even if you put all the advice in this book into practice, you will still experience some issues with behaviour. It's human nature you're dealing with, after all, in all its majestic complexity.

This is where being persistent comes in:

- Don't give up on the strategies because they don't work immediately.
- Remember, all the time you are working on your behaviour management skills, you are becoming a more effective teacher.

- Every time something goes wrong, see this as a learning opportunity – do things differently next time round.

In some schools, where getting appropriate behaviour is a constant battle, there will be days when you feel like throwing in the towel. It is very tempting indeed to give up on your key expectations, simply because there is so much disruption going on that you don't know where to begin. But the moment that the learners see you thinking 'talk while I talk; I don't care' or 'it doesn't matter if you're disrespectful', then you are effectively giving up on them, and on the values you hold true.

Sometimes you may come across 'the class from hell': a class which, for some reason, contains a high number of learners who are really struggling with behaviour, or an unbalanced mix. Again, it's very hard to keep going, to keep plugging away at behaviour and insisting on certain standards, but you have to try. Similarly, some children will apparently throw all your efforts straight back in your face. Never lose sight of the fact that some learners face really challenging circumstances outside of school. Try as hard as you can not to give up on the learner who always pushes you away, but accept that you can't change the world for everyone.

Engage them

'I want you to want to learn.'

When things are going well, it's relatively easy to find interesting ideas for learning, and to feel inspired about your planning. It's not so easy when your class is difficult to manage, or when learners are behaving inappropriately. But this is the time when it is most crucial. 'Engaging them' is about finding activities that make your learners feel interested, excited, curious, puzzled, amused, or just generally in the right frame of mind to learn. This is *not* to say that every lesson you ever teach should be an all-singing, all-dancing festival of fun. Nor am I saying that if your learners behave inappropriately it is your fault for not making the lesson engaging enough – their behaviour is still *their* behaviour. But your approach to teaching and learning is one of the areas over which you have most control, and when you do interest and enthuse your learners, you are *more likely* to encourage them to behave properly. At the very least, it's got to be worth a try.

To engage your learners, it helps to:

- get creative with what goes on in your lessons
- find ways to make the learning feel enjoyable when you can
- be brave enough to try original, experimental activities and to take some risks
- use interesting, engaging, multisensory resources
- think laterally about how to present new concepts and ideas.

Think carefully about what holds you back from being more experimental, and how you might deal with these concerns. Are you worried about:

- what others will think?
- the learners getting overexcited?
- making too much noise or mess?
- the class getting out of control?
- the pressures of accountability?

Consider ahead of time how you would deal with these issues. Ask yourself: 'What is the worst that could happen?' and then work to pre-empt these problems. Clearly, you don't want to put yourself or your learners at unnecessary risk, but at the same time you've got to put your trust in them if you want to make progress with learning and behaviour. For lots more on the link between high-quality learning and behaviour, see Chapter 7.

Chapter 2
Managing the First Meeting

Why is the first meeting so important?

Your first meeting with any class offers you the chance to sow the seeds for a successful year, or to take the first step on the road to disaster. Every teacher surely knows that hollow feeling in the pit of the stomach, as you invite a new class into your room, aware that what you do in that first meeting will have such a long-term impact. Often, both the teacher and the learners are at their most nervous or defensive in the first lesson (in secondary) or during the first day together (in primary). You may be anticipating challenging behaviour from a 'difficult' group; they may be expecting you to dislike them if they know that other teachers have found them to be a problem.

In an early years setting, your first meeting is often with an individual child, rather than with a whole class or group. The connection you make when you first meet a child and their parents or carers is vital in establishing a positive ongoing relationship. Home visits are very useful to build your knowledge of the family's needs. In school-based education settings you will obviously meet with your new class, or with all your new classes, at the start of the school year. Making contacts with parents and carers can typically happen fairly quickly in primaries, but can be more of a long-term aim in secondary schools.

With some classes, the first few meetings offer you a 'honeymoon period', where your learners are getting to know you, checking you out before revealing their behaviour in full. It's good advice not to start out with an overly relaxed attitude (although this is hard when you're new to teaching). If you are too laid-back you may find that, a few lessons into the year, the learners start to push at the boundaries and it's hard to backtrack.

Sometimes you can find yourself in a situation where the learners behave inappropriately because you are the new teacher, testing you to see whether you can withstand the ordeal. This makes life difficult: it's hard to establish your expectations of behaviour with a class that refuses to listen. If you find yourself in this situation, turn to others to help and support you, for instance, asking a member of the leadership team to be present in the room while you talk about your expectations.

What do you need to know before the first meeting?

Teachers are put in a difficult position at the start of a school year (or at the start of the term, if you begin your job midway through the year). They are expected to meet, control and teach a group of young people about whom they know little or nothing. Because of this, there can be a tendency to learn through mistakes, dealing with problems as they arise, rather than anticipating them and trying to resolve them beforehand.

Time is in short supply at the start of term, with staff busy setting up their rooms, planning, emptying in-trays, and so on. However, this first meeting with your new group is so important that it pays to take some time out to prepare. Before you meet a new class, you could find out about:

- **Potential behaviour issues:** are there well-known 'characters' in the class? If you know that learner's name, and what is likely to set them off, you can keep an eye out for the early signs of boundary testing. Make sure you give everyone the chance of a fresh start, though: judge them solely on how they behave for you. Sometimes, older learners claim to be proud of having a reputation. Try turning this situation on its head: 'Jason, great to meet you – I've heard so many good things about you. I'm really looking forward to working with you.'

- **Learning needs:** find out whether any learners have special educational needs or disabilities (SEND) that could have an impact on their learning and potentially on their behaviour. You should be given a list of those children with SEND and details of what these needs are.

  If you are not, approach your special educational needs coordinator (SENCO) for this information. If you're not aware of a specific learning need, you might wrongly perceive it as a behavioural issue. For instance, a learner with weak literacy skills may not complete the work set in the time available. This could be interpreted as a 'poor attitude to learning' unless the teacher understands the background to the situation.

- **Physical needs:** find out about any learners with physical difficulties or disabilities so you can take these into consideration. Don't assume that learners are confident enough to tell you about their needs, particularly if you work with younger children. Physical needs could include learners who have hearing difficulties or a visual impairment. Adapt seating arrangements for learners who need to be close to the front of the room. Take account of children who are left-handed too (about 20 per cent of the population). Don't seat a child who is left-handed on the right side of a child who is right-handed, because they will bump elbows.

- **Some names:** it's very useful to know the names of some of your learners before you meet them. Even better, if you're good at memory tricks, learn the names of the whole class, and claim to be a magician ('Is there a Joe in this class? And a Jasdeep?'). Knowing your learners' names is vital for handling behaviour: so start learning them right away. I've included some ideas for how to learn names in Chapter 2 under 'Learning names', page 30.

While pursuing knowledge is very useful, never prejudge a class. This could put you in a negative frame of mind for the first encounter. It's also unfair on the learners. Some learners who gain a bad reputation early on never get a chance to prove this reputation false. Tell your class you hope they will impress you – you may be pleasantly surprised.

Establishing your teaching style

The more experienced you become as a teacher, the clearer you get about the teaching style you want to use. A fully developed teaching style is something that comes with time and practice. But before you meet a class for the first time, have at least some idea about the style of teaching you want to use. From the first moment they meet you, your learners will make decisions about you, based on the signals you send through your teaching style.

Adapt the style you use according to your individual work situation. There are many possible variables to consider: the type and ethos of the school or setting, the learners' age, your own personality, and so on. I explore the concept of effective teaching and useful teaching styles in lots of detail in Chapters 4 and 5. In your first meeting, some areas will be under immediate examination:

- How you appear: are you smart, wearing a suit, or do you dress casually? (Either may be fine, depending on the appropriate attire for your age group and context.) Are you ready to meet and teach your class, or flustered and bad tempered when they arrive? Interviewers make snap judgements about candidates in the first few minutes of an interview, based mainly on how they look; similarly, if you want your class to behave, you need to make a good impression at this first meeting.

- The way you talk: do you sound relaxed or stressed out when you speak? Does your voice sound timid, confident or too loud? Do you use variations of tone and pace to give interest to what you say? Our voices tell others a huge amount about our emotional state, especially when we are tense or under pressure.

- The way you stand and move: are you relaxed and making good use of the space? Or do you stand frozen at the front, backed up against the wall in a defensive posture? Does your body language signal aggression or self-confidence? Your learners will be reading these signals subconsciously to help them decide how to behave for you.

- The way you treat your learners: do you see your learners as equals, or do you have an authoritarian manner? Do you respect people and talk to them politely, maintaining a good example, whatever the provocation? Do you stay calm when handling incidents? Remember, when you deal with individual learners, the others watch to see how you handle them. Your learners are making conscious and subconscious decisions, based on what they see, about how they might behave for you in the future.

- The way you start and finish sessions: are you prepared and waiting, with a starter activity already organised? Or are you flustered and running late, trying to log into the computer? Do you run out of time at the end of the lesson and let the class rush out of the room when the bell goes? Or does your session end in a controlled way? Do you put the learners in a good mood from the first minute they meet you? Do they leave you feeling that they have had a positive experience, one they want to repeat?

- The way you teach: are the activities varied, interesting, challenging and fun? Or do you talk for far too long, so the learners get bored and start to mess around? I know you can't make every single lesson totally engaging, but try hard to make at least some of them great. If you captivate your learners early on, they will come to your class in a constructive frame of mind, ready and eager to learn.

- The way you keep control: with only one of you and lots of learners, you need to take control of the situation. But how do you go about doing this? Are you a 'strict and scary' teacher, loud from the first moment you meet the class? Are you 'firm but fair', controlling them through the strength of your personality? Or perhaps you're 'comic and quirky', the kind of 'character' teacher they're going to have fun with? For more on different teaching styles, take a look at Chapter 5.

Establishing your expectations

Having clear expectations, and sharing these with your class, is a key factor in effective behaviour management. In the first few meetings you are defining the boundaries: 'this is acceptable behaviour and this is not'. Or, to put it another way: 'here's a line, just make sure you don't step over it'. By establishing your expectations, you show that you are fully in charge of your classroom or teaching space. Your learners want and indeed appreciate a sense of certainty and clarity from you about what is required. If you are new to teaching, it is a really good idea to practise your 'first lesson speech' *before* you meet your class or classes for the first time. Do it out loud, filming yourself, or trial it on a friend. The idea is to come across clear, confident, and without any umms or errs.

As explained in Chapter 1, an excellent way to explain your expectations is to make statements about what you want or need – the appropriate behaviours for learning. Phrase your statements in the right way for the age group you're working with – use your professional judgement to decide what will work best. Choose three expectations to have of your learners for the first time you meet them, perhaps spending some time talking together about why it's important for them to do these things. Your statements could be:

Early years/lower primary

- 'We always listen to each other.'
- 'We walk; we don't run.'
- 'We are kind to each other and we share.'

Upper primary/lower secondary

- 'I expect you to pay silent attention when someone is addressing the whole group.'
- 'I expect you to stay in your seats, unless you have permission to get up.'
- 'I expect you to give it a go and try your hardest.'

Upper secondary/further education

- 'I need you all to listen, so we can get on with learning.'
- 'I want to see respectful attitudes from everyone.'
- 'I need to hear appropriate language at all times.'

The way you phrase these statements is a question of personal taste, style and judgement. As you gain experience, you'll find it gets easier to decide how you want to do it.

High expectations are a powerful tool in gaining appropriate behaviour and hard work from your learners, because they demonstrate your faith in the potential of every single member of your class. There's an excellent example of this in the film

Dangerous Minds. The teacher (played by Michelle Pfeiffer) begins her first lesson by telling her class of disaffected learners that they all have a grade 'A'. When this statement is greeted with shouts of derision, she explains that they *do* all have an 'A', it's just that it's up to *them* whether they choose to keep it or to throw it away. To establish your expectations effectively:

- **Use clear, specific statements:** give positive targets of what you want the learners to do, rather than negative statements about what you don't.

- **Describe the behaviour:** when you ask for silent attention, be clear what it looks like – eyes to the front, focusing, listening to what is said. Be clear in your own mind what your expectation looks like, and let your learners know too.

- **Discuss what you expect:** spend time talking *with* (not *at*) the class about what you want. Ask your learners what they think acceptable behaviour is and why it's needed.

- **Not too many at once:** don't give out long lists of demands in your first lesson – your learners won't retain them. Work out your key expectations and get these in place first.

- **Refer back to them:** talk about your expectations repeatedly – at the end of the session, at the start of the next, every time you see someone meeting them. Revisit your expectations every time you can to reinforce them.

- **Use a 'drip-feed' approach:** introduce further expectations as appropriate over the next few meetings. Link your expectations with an activity – for instance, the first time you do group work, establish the behaviour that you expect from learners when they are working in this format.

- **Match your phrasing to the group:** adapt your explanation to fit the age/attitude of your learners. Be as firm as you can get away with in your particular age group. Don't terrify them, but don't come across as a soft touch either. With young learners, be very clear and simple; with older ones, take a more subtle approach.

- **Model what you're after:** as well as *telling* the learners what you want, you absolutely must *show* them by your own behaviour. If you've asked for silence, you can't talk over them. Otherwise, you are effectively telling them that you don't actually mean what you say.

Establishing the pattern of your lessons/days

The first lesson is a stressful experience for both teacher and learners, because there are so many unknown factors. You've not yet built up a relationship with the group, and theoretically 'anything could happen'. To make the situation feel more controlled and manageable, and to help your learners feel secure, you must establish a clear structure or pattern. At secondary or further education level, this means creating a pattern to each lesson; in early years or primary, it means finding a structure for your days. Do this as soon as you can and make a start in your first meeting.

You can establish a pattern for many different aspects of your hourly or daily routine. Consider the following questions to help you work out the best structure for you and your class:

- How do your learners enter at the start of the lesson/day?
- Where do you stand when the learners are entering?
- What do you do while the learners come in?
- What do the learners do once they're in the room?
- How does the day or lesson start?
- At what point during your time together do you take the register?
- How much talking is allowed during individual activities?
- How do you manage handing out and collecting in resources?
- How does the session finish?
- How do the learners leave the room?

As you can see, there are lots of individual decisions to make before you can fully establish the 'pattern' of your lessons. Probably the best way to illustrate what I mean by a 'pattern' is to give an example. Below you'll find an account of one way of doing things in a lower-secondary English lesson, lasting one hour. I've given a commentary to show why the teacher uses this pattern, or set of structures.

Example lesson

9.00 am – the bell goes. Mr Charman checks that everything is ready, then goes to wait outside the room, closing the door behind him.

Comment: the teacher begins the lesson by standing outside the room, with the door closed. This creates a physical and psychological barrier between the learners and the space.

9.03 am – the learners arrive in dribs and drabs. Mr Charman stays waiting for them at the door, arms folded. He appears relaxed but ready. As they turn up, he calmly directs individuals to line up, in single file, until everyone arrives, praising those who are in correct uniform.

Comment: the pattern for lessons is being set. The class will line up outside the room until they have all arrived, a useful classroom management technique for this age group. As yet, Mr Charman has not addressed the whole class. He is waiting to do this until most of the learners have arrived.

9.07 am – Mr Charman looks very deliberately at his watch and clears his throat. He is now ready to begin. He gets the learners silent, then talks to them briefly about what they should do as they enter the room. He wants bags under desks, pencil cases out, and then everyone facing the front, ready to listen.

Comment: the teacher has been lenient with the time, so as not to set up confrontations at the start of his first lesson. He'll explain his exact requirements for future punctuality once the class is settled.

9.12 am – the learners are settled in their seats. Mr Charman waits for a moment until they fall silent, using non-verbal signals to get their full attention. He begins by explaining how his lessons will run. He sets his three main boundaries and makes it clear why these are important. He alludes to his encyclopaedic knowledge of the school consequences policy, in case anyone might choose to misbehave.

Comment: although the teacher will normally move quickly into the teaching and learning part of his lessons, during this first meeting he wants to establish his expectations. He makes his boundaries very clear, while his learners are at their most receptive.

9.17 am – Mr Charman reminds the class of his expectation of silent attention when someone is talking. He explains to the class that he likes to start his lessons by checking who is present. He tells the learners what the consequence will be for lateness. He then takes the register.

Comment: taking the register at the start of lessons is a matter of personal taste and the teaching situation you're in. In some schools or with some age groups, it would not be sensible or useful to aim to do this – better to get the learners straight onto an activity, then take the register once they are settled on task. In some age groups, for instance, in early years, children might self-register when they arrive.

9.20 am – next Mr Charman needs to sort out exercise books. He explains to the learners that, when they get their book, they should write their name, subject, class and teacher on the front. He writes this information up on his interactive whiteboard.

Comment: in your first few lessons, be very clear about these details – what do they write, how do they write it, what do they write with? Establish what you expect early on.

9.22 am – having finished his explanation, Mr Charman pre-empts any problems with a lack of writing materials by asking for 'hands up' from anyone who doesn't have a pen. Three learners have turned up without their equipment. As he moves around the room handing pens to these learners, he tells them that this must be a one-off. He explains that, in future, anyone arriving without a pen will get an automatic consequence. He asks for two volunteers to hand out the new books and chooses learners who have been listening well. He also sets a time limit of three minutes to get this task done, so that they can get on with the 'lesson proper'.

Comment: think ahead about potential issues that might crop up. Notice here how Mr Charman has planned for those who might not have pens. He also chooses volunteers who are following his expectations already, thus setting up the chance to volunteer as a reward. In your first meeting with a class, there are often various bits of 'admin' to get done. Be clear about your exact requirements to save yourself time and stress.

9.25 am – all the learners have got their books sorted. Now Mr Charman brings out five items – a pack of playing cards, a football scarf, a CD, a trowel and a map of Spain. He explains that he wants to get to know them a bit better. Each of these items has a close connection to his life – what do they think those connections could be? They discuss this in pairs and give some suggestions as a whole class. Next he asks them to turn to the person sitting next to them, and talk about five items that have a connection to *their* lives.

Comment: Mr Charman is setting up a quick activity that will give him an insight into his learners' interests. He also wants to give them a brief insight into who he is. By using engaging resources to start the activity, he hooks them into it. He understands they have been sitting listening for a while, so he uses talk partners to liven things up.

9.30 am – Mr Charman asks for hands up (establishing this expectation) from anyone who would like to explain what they chose and why. He gets the learners to share their ideas, all the time reinforcing that they must wait for silent attention before they address the class.

Comment: the teacher gets all the learners to share their ideas, while at the same time reinforcing his expectations of their behaviour.

9.40 am – Mr Charman sets a brief written task: 'My life in five items'. Before they begin, he clarifies how written tasks will be done: title, date, neat handwriting, care with spelling, and so on.

Comment: Mr Charman wants to get a short sample of each learner's writing, so he sets them a quick written task to finish off the lesson. The pattern of his lessons has been set. He will start by explaining the aim of the lesson; there will be plenty of variety in the type of tasks chosen and the pace of the learning; he will try to keep his learners' interest throughout.

9.53 am – Mr Charman stops the class, gets silence, and then explains the pattern for the end of lessons. The learners will write their homework down and clear away equipment one table at a time.

Comment: the teacher has left plenty of time so that the end of his first lesson is calm and well managed.

9.57 am – the learners have put the resources away. Mr Charman gets silence, then asks them to stand behind their chairs. He praises them for the excellent work they have done.

Comment: by ending early, Mr Charman has time to praise his learners. He sets up a good feeling about this first lesson together. He also has time to host a plenary, to make clear his expectations about homework, or answer any last-minute queries.

10.00 am – when the bell goes, Mr Charman lets the best-behaved and hardest-working learners go first, praising them as they leave.

Comment: to finish, the teacher shows how to earn the 'reward' of going first – by working hard and behaving sensibly. The learners leave with a good first impression of a well-structured, well-managed lesson.

Learning names

From the moment we're born, our names are a fundamental part of what makes us who we are. Even if you don't particularly like your name, it's still inextricably linked to you and your interactions with the world. Learning and using names is a very powerful way to build relationships and manage behaviour. By using someone's name, you show your awareness of the individuals in your class, and you demonstrate respect for them as people. As any supply teacher will attest, when you're trying to control behaviour, you are at a great disadvantage if you do not know the names.

Once you know names, you can use them to:

- get a learner's attention
- personalise a reward
- highlight a learner who is working particularly well
- give a consequence
- refer a learner to the relevant senior leader
- build positive relationships.

Unfortunately, there's no magical shortcut to learning names. It's clearly easier in the early years setting, and at primary school, where you work mainly with one reasonably small group of learners. However, at secondary or further education levels, you could teach literally hundreds of different learners. If that's the case for you, use every technique you can think of to make the process quicker and smoother. Incorporate some or all of the ideas below into your first meeting with each group.

You could:

- **Use memory systems:** memory systems are useful for learning names. The basic idea is to create 'hooks' or connections between things (do a search online or see Tony Buzan's books for more on memory techniques). To give one example, you could link a learner called David with a well-known footballer in your mind.

- **Make notes on your register:** a few subtle annotations on your class list can help you learn names. Make a brief note of any distinguishing characteristics (such as a learner who wears glasses).

- **Set yourself a target:** the task of learning names can feel insurmountable, especially if you teach hundreds of different learners. Set yourself a target: five or so names per lesson. Within a few weeks you will have learnt the names of all your learners (or a few days in a primary class).

- **Do name games and activities:** spend time doing name-specific activities in your first couple of lessons. Ask your learners to make decorated nameplates to sit on their desks, or to wear sticky name labels. Get them to write an acrostic poem, using the first letters of their names to start each line. Ask them to talk about their name to the class: whether they like it, who chose it, what country it is from, why they were called this, and so on.

- **Focus on the quiet ones:** when you're teaching a class with a number of learners in it who behave poorly, it is tempting to focus on the most disruptive, learning their names first. Focus on getting to know the names of some quiet learners in your first meeting as well.

And of course…

- **Use a seating plan:** this is a great way of learning names, and it's also useful for establishing control. With a seating plan in place, you send a definite signal about your style – structured, orderly, in charge. Use 'being allowed to sit where you want' as a reward for consistent appropriate behaviour.

If you're new to teaching, it's tough to get a seating plan in place while dealing with all the other stresses of the first meeting. But if you don't do it in the first lesson, it is much harder later on. There are various different methods for getting a seating plan in place, so ask your colleagues for advice. For instance, you might:

- Draw a plan and stick it on the wall for the learners to follow.
- Let the learners in one by one, seating them as you go.
- Get the learners to line up in register order before coming in to be seated.

If you're not comfortable about getting a seating plan in place in your first lesson, get one of the learners to draw you a plan once everyone is seated. This is also a useful technique when doing supply teaching.

Reducing the stress of the first meeting

Although the first lesson can be stressful, remember that, as yet, these children or young people have formed little or no opinion of you. If you are an old hand at your school, your reputation will precede you, particularly if there are siblings of learners you have already taught in the class. If you are a new teacher at the school, you are currently the 'mystery teacher', an unknown entity, and consequently of great interest. Older learners have an uncanny ability to identify (and subsequently to be difficult for) trainee teachers. If that's you, prepare a convincing response to the question: 'Are you a student teacher?'

If you experience problems in your first lesson, your confidence might drop. If this happens:

- **Stay calm and relaxed:** if you get tense and angry, you give your learners an incentive to misbehave in future. Breathe deeply and stay as calm as you can.
- **React from the head:** make a conscious decision to react intellectually, rather than emotionally. Don't let your heart win the day – there's no point in getting upset or angry.
- **Don't get defensive:** remind yourself that it's not personal. If your learners 'attack' your lesson by behaving poorly, refuse to respond by becoming hostile in return. It's far more helpful to stay relentlessly positive.

And if all else fails…

- **Don't be a perfectionist:** it's not a total disaster if a few learners muck around in your first lesson. The world is not going to end. You're not going to get the sack. And you'll learn some valuable lessons from the experience.

Chapter 3
Key Strategies and Techniques

How do I establish and maintain boundaries?

Before I give you some 'key strategies and techniques' for managing your class, it's worth considering why you need to establish boundaries to control behaviour in the first place. Obviously, it's important for safety reasons, but the main reason appropriate behaviour is needed is so that everyone can get on with learning. Understanding how to establish boundaries is not about being a control freak, it's done simply so that you can teach. The more strategies you have at your disposal to achieve this, the more confident you will feel. When things are going wrong, you can try one approach after another, until you find something that works.

Controlling a large group of people is difficult in any situation, but when some of your learners have no wish to be in school, let alone in your lesson, life can be very tough. In addition to using the key principles described in Chapter 1, there are many other methods that will help you create and maintain an orderly, relaxed atmosphere in your classroom. The ten strategies described on the following pages are easy to understand and apply, and should cost you little in the way of stress.

1 Learn to 'read and respond'

There are many factors that can affect the behaviour of a class, or of the individuals within that group. These factors include:

- the time of day
- the day of the week
- the weather (watch out for rain, snow and very hot days)
- the presence or absence of certain individuals
- what happened in the previous lesson

- any incidents at break or lunchtime
- the teaching space you are working in
- the topic area you are covering
- the activities you are using
- your mood or emotional state
- outside events (e.g. a local football match that evening).

You can hype up your class, and equally you can calm them down. Sometimes you'll catch yourself getting the learners overexcited, and you should take measures to bring down the excitement levels. This effect is particularly vivid with young children: even the way your voice sounds is enough to get some groups over-excited. You can also have the same effect on individual learners, particularly when you are dealing with behaviour.

The ability to 'read and respond' to a class or an individual, by adapting what you do in the moment, is a subtle skill to learn. You also need to be open to the idea that behaviour is a form of communication – that it can provide useful feedback on your approach. It involves using the flexibility discussed in the first chapter. This technique comes more easily with experience, and also as you get to know your class and the people within it. To 'read and respond', you need to:

- Make on-the-spot judgements throughout the lesson.
- Base these judgements on how learners respond to the activities you're doing, and also on how well your behaviour strategies are working.
- Adapt or even throw away a lesson activity if it's not going well.
- Change your behaviour management techniques if necessary.
- Be particularly flexible on days when there are already high levels of tension in the class.

This technique is especially important for supply and cover teachers. It's also vital if you have someone with a 'short fuse' in your class. Don't lower your standards, but use your professional judgement to make decisions about the right balance between consistency and flexibility.

2 Wait for silence

This is one of the most important techniques a teacher can use to encourage and enhance learning. When I say 'wait for silence', I don't mean you should get your learners silent and then talk at them endlessly. Nor do I mean you should always simply *wait*. What I mean is this: when you need to talk to the whole class you should not address the learners until they are silent and focused on you, or on whoever is speaking. This applies at the start of the day or lesson, for instance, when taking the register, and also at any time when you talk to the whole class. When you get silent attention:

- You send a clear message: the learning is important and you will not allow it to be jeopardised.
- The learners can hear the explanations, instructions or ideas.
- It shows respect to whoever is speaking and is just basic courtesy.
- Listening well is a skill that many learners need to practise.

Remember, if you give up, and let the learners talk over you, you are basically saying: 'Go ahead and talk; I don't mind.' If you work with very young children, you may only get a few minutes of silence at a time. With adults, you can expect longer (although even adults have a threshold and will drift off if you don't spice things up with other approaches). A useful rule of thumb with children is to speak for a maximum of about 'their age plus two', before you change tack and do something different, i.e. five minutes for a three-year-old, ten minutes for an eight-year-old, and so on. Of course, that is not to say that you *have* to use up all that time with talk. Nor is it to say that you can only ever speak for this amount of time. If you need to talk for longer, divide up the talk with a chance for the learners to discuss their ideas, to give responses or to do a quick activity to try something out.

In your quest to get silence, it is best to use non-verbal, rather than verbal, techniques. These create less stress for you and add less noise to your classroom. They also give a sense of control and confidence. There is little more ineffective than the teacher shouting over a noisy class 'Be quiet! Be quiet!' in an increasingly loud voice. You can find some age-specific strategies for getting silent attention in Chapters 11 and 12. Here are a few approaches that can be adapted for most age groups:

- **The force of your personality:** if the class is reasonably well behaved, try standing with your arms folded, looking ready or, if necessary, mean. Hold your nerve and refuse to begin speaking until there is silence. Look around, raise an eyebrow, and use as many subtle non-verbal cues as you can. If this technique is going to work (and it might not), it will do so within a couple of minutes at most.

- **The power of the pause:** in teaching, you quickly learn that there's a lot of waiting. When you are in the middle of talking to the class, and an individual begins to talk, use a pause to indicate that you want silence. Similarly, if a learner is addressing the whole class, and someone begins to talk over them, ask them to pause and to 'wait for silence' just like you. There's no need to even identify who was talking when you do this – use the power of the pause to communicate the message. At first it may feel like you are wasting lots of time, but eventually you will train your learners in the behaviour you need.

- **Visual cues:** you can add a visual element to your pauses by using an egg timer. Every time you have to wait for the class, turn the timer over so that some sand runs through. Once the learners fall silent, turn the timer on its side so that the sand remains in place. This gives a visual indication of time wasted. Ask that the learners 'earn' this time back, for instance, through working in silence for a while.

- **The non-verbal 'silence signal':** a pre-agreed non-verbal signal is a great way to achieve silence. It is essential in some subjects or situations (for instance, in a PE or drama lesson, where the learners may be engaged in a noisy activity or spread around a large open space). When a group of young children are engrossed in a game, and less aware of any non-verbal signals, try using a sound such as a bell or shaker instead. Train your class to respond quickly to your chosen signal, practising and praising the learners when they get it right. Turn this into a game or challenge, to make it fun for younger learners to join in – how quickly can they react? To give your 'silence signal' you might:
  - blow a whistle or ring a bell
  - rap three times on a desk
  - clap in a pattern, which the learners must copy
  - raise a hand – everyone else must stop and raise their hands too
  - sit in your 'silent seat'
  - stand on your 'silent spot'
  - do a little boogie (embarrassing but gets their attention).
  - Use an aural cue. I once met a teacher who had trained his primary class to respond to various tunes on a xylophone. He had a tune for 'fall silent', another for 'line up', another for 'put your resources away', and so on.

- **The well-chosen phrase:** with some classes a verbal cue for silence is effective. Pitch your voice at a fairly quiet volume. Here are some age-specific phrases to try:
  - 3–5 years: 'Let's see fingers on lips, everyone; that's great'.
  - 5+ years: 'Looking this way and listening carefully in 3, 2, 1, thanks'.
  - 11+ years: 'I need complete silence before I continue'.
  - 15+ years: 'C'mon guys, everyone listening now, please'.
  - Any age: 'Let's have silence in 5… 4… 3… 2…1.'

- **The 'broken record' technique:** if your learners don't respond immediately to your well-chosen phrase, this technique is fun and effective. Repeat your phrase over and over again, stopping midway through, until the learners respond.

Talk about your expectation of there being 'one voice' in your first lesson with a class. Get the learners to think about why this boundary is so important. Model the behaviour you're after – listen carefully to your learners when they talk, use facial expressions to show you are listening, and try never to talk over a class.

If you find that you simply can't get the learners to be silent, particularly at the start of a lesson, think laterally to get around the problem. Perhaps you should plunge them straight into an engaging starter activity instead? Maybe you could get one of the learners to help you mark off names on the register, or ask them to self-register? It's better to write messages to your class on your board, than to talk over children who don't intend to listen.

3 Make use of cues

A lot of teacher stress is caused by low-level behaviours that are inappropriate for a classroom context – learners calling out answers rather than putting their hands up, or starting an activity before you've finished explaining it. The idea behind the use of cues is to pre-empt the issue arising in the first place. Encourage the learners to behave as you need them to, rather than waiting for them to make an error then telling them off. You can use cues for any behaviour that is repeated regularly, and they can be verbal or non-verbal. Cues often change over time, becoming a form of shorthand understood by all. Here are a couple of examples to show what I mean:

- **Answering questions:** start any whole-class question with the phrase: 'Put your hand up if you can tell me...' By specifying the behaviour you want (hands up), you anticipate and overcome the incorrect response (calling out). This can gradually be abbreviated to 'Hands up' or just a slight raise of your hand. Alternatively, you could use other strategies to avoid the issue of calling out ever arising, for instance, using talk partners and then asking a random learner to share their pair's answer.
- **Giving instructions:** some keen learners want to start work before you finish giving the instructions; others don't want to start at all. Use the phrase 'When I say "go" I want you to...' to pre-empt this. Once you've finished your explanation, set the class off to work by saying '3, 2, 1, go.' Again, this becomes a shorthand, with the question 'Did I say go yet?' making clear that it wasn't yet time to start.

4 Give them 'the choice'

We cannot actually *force* our learners to behave – we can only make it seem like the best of all possible options. Ideally, we want them to take responsibility for their own actions, and for the consequences of those actions. This helps create a positive and effective environment for learning. It is also vital in setting them up for their lives beyond education, when the choices they make about behaviour become much more crucial ('Should I go with my friends to rob that house or not?').

This is where the technique of 'the choice' comes in. There are essentially two choices: either the learners do as you reasonably ask, or they will need to accept the consequences of a refusal to cooperate. You need to get on with teaching and learning – if their behaviour makes that impossible, you can utilise the behaviour system to give a consequence. This is only fair on the majority who *do* want to learn. If we make the choices and consequences simple and clear, this can prevent inappropriate behaviours from escalating. You encourage learners to consider and change their negative behaviours, to avoid unwelcome consequences in the future.

'The choice' helps you depersonalise a range of tricky situations, because it puts responsibility in the hands of the learner. It is up to them to decide how they wish to behave, and which consequences they are willing to receive. Your role is almost like that of 'police officer' – applying the code of conduct of the place where you work.

When using 'the choice':

- State the behaviour you require.
- Make clear the positive benefits of doing as you ask.
- Make clear the consequences within the school system of refusing to comply.
- Give the learner a short time to consider their decision.
- If they choose not to cooperate, explain that you will have to apply the consequences.
- Aim to sound disappointed, rather than vengeful.

Let's look at a couple of examples of a teacher using 'the choice', to see how it works.

For example...

Reception-age learners

Tiffany is pushing other children in the role-play area. The teacher has just seen her grab a doll from Hafiz and now he is crying.

Teacher: [*bobbing down beside Tiffany to talk with her*] Tiffany, I need you to play nicely and stop pushing the other children. Give the doll back to Hafiz now please.

Tiffany: [*holding it tight*] Won't! It's mine.

Teacher: Tiffany, I want you to give it back to Hafiz now, or I'll have to take it and ask you to leave the role play area. That would be a shame, wouldn't it?

Tiffany: No, I won't give it back. I want to play with it.

Teacher: [*deciding to use a distraction to back up 'the choice'*]
Oh look! Hafiz has got a buggy for the doll. Pop it in the buggy, Tiffany, and then why don't you come and do some painting with me?

At this point Tiffany will either do as she's asked, or the teacher will take the doll from her and lead her away from the area.

Learners of 13+ years

Sarah is in a terrible mood. As she enters the classroom, she shoves her way past a group of girls, pushing one of them to the floor.

Teacher: Sarah! That's unacceptable behaviour. [*Pointing to the door*] I want you to come outside with me right now, please, so we can discuss this and you can make an apology to Ana.

Sarah: Nah, I won't. Are you gonna make me?

Teacher: [*The teacher moves in close to speak to Sarah without the rest of the learners hearing.*] Sarah. You have a choice. Come outside with me right now so we can sort this out. If you refuse, I will have to send for a senior leader to remove you from my lesson. And I really don't want to do that. I'll wait for you by the door while you decide.

Again, at this point, Sarah will either comply or the teacher will follow through with the consequences as described.

5 Be reasonable, but don't reason with them

I was given this tip by a headteacher in a Scottish primary school, and it struck me as a wonderful summary of an effective and balanced approach to teacher/learner (and also parent/child) relationships. So long as you are reasonable with your learners, and you don't have unrealistic expectations about how they will work or behave, there is no need to constantly reason with them over what you ask them to do.

Here are some examples of how this works with different age groups:

For example...

Early years

It's perfectly reasonable to insist children don't paint on the walls. *So long as you don't* get cross about the odd splash on the floor.

Primary

It's perfectly reasonable to have silence to explain an activity. *So long as you don't* take 15 minutes to explain it.

Secondary

It's perfectly reasonable to ask learners to write in silence. *So long as you don't* expect them to write silently for hours at a time.

Further education

It's perfectly reasonable to insist that mobile phones are kept in bags. *So long as you don't* remove a phone from a learner whose parent is in hospital.

When inappropriate behaviour is challenged, learners often try to drag you into a discussion, rather than accept responsibility for what they have done. Some learners are clever at deflecting the teacher's challenge, and it is important to learn to stick to your guns. Refuse to get drawn into endless debates about 'whose fault it was' or 'why I can't do this'. The 'being reasonable' part of the equation is tricky to manage – you need to make decisions about the right balance to strike. Set high standards, and expect the best, but be realistic. If you are too authoritarian with your demands, confrontations and difficulties may arise. If you are too reasonable and relaxed, learners may take advantage.

6 Use statements, not questions, and assume compliance

Asking rhetorical questions to manage behaviour is a common mistake. Here's the classic scenario:

Learner: You're a 'f*****g b*****d'!
Teacher: [*horrified*] What did you say?
Learner: I said, 'you're a f*****g b*****d!'

I suspect it might be a matter of habit – as teachers we frequently use questions, so we get used to this vocal style. To help you overcome the habit, follow this rule of thumb: 'never ask a question if you don't want to get an answer'.

Use statements about what you want, rather than questions about what you don't. This is much more helpful for your learners – you state what they should be doing, rather than complain about what they are not. It gives the impression of someone who knows what they want, and who has confidence that the children will do it for them. Of course, in some situations a question is appropriate and you want to receive an answer. For instance, asking a child: 'Is there something the matter today?' or 'How can I support you with this?' might be a good starting point for a discussion about starting work on a learning task.

Here are a few examples of questions rephrased as statements:

- 'Why aren't you doing the work?' becomes 'I need you to get on with the activity now, so you can leave on time.'

- 'Why are you being so silly?' becomes 'I want you to sit properly on your chair and focus on the learning, thanks.'

- 'Why aren't you listening?' becomes 'Everyone looking this way and listening in silence, thank you.'

When you're making positive statements about what you want, you can also use a technique called 'assumed compliance'. This means that you say 'thanks' (you assume they'll do it) rather than 'please' (you hope they will). If you use statements and assume compliance simultaneously, you will sound like a teacher who is positive, certain and confident about getting what they want.

7 Use repetition

Much of the time, when we say something, we expect it to be heard and understood the first time around. This is not necessarily a sensible expectation. It can lead to unnecessary misunderstandings and confrontations. Classrooms can be noisy and confusing places for learners: there can be many reasons why they do not respond immediately to your directions or instructions. You might usefully use repetition with your learners:

- to get their attention before you give an instruction
- to ensure they are listening if you need to warn them about a potential consequence
- because they might not hear your instructions the first time you give them
- to clarify any possible misunderstandings and make your wishes clear
- to reinforce your instructions and make it clear that they must be followed
- to support understanding for learners for whom English is not their first language.

Repetition is particularly helpful when you have to give a consequence to a learner. In this situation, you might repeat:

- their name, to get their attention
- the instruction you have given or the behaviour you want (ask the learner to repeat this, to check for understanding)
- the options for avoiding a consequence
- the consequence you are giving, if the learner fails to cooperate.

Here's an example of how you can use repetition to deal with behaviour. Alice is chatting to her friends instead of working.

For example...

Teacher: Alice. [*The teacher waits; there is no response.*]
Teacher: Alice. I'd like you to look at me and listen, thanks.
Alice: What, Miss? [*She is still looking at her friends.*]
Teacher: Alice. I said I want you to look at me and listen.

Finally, she turns around and looks at the teacher.

Teacher: Thank you, Alice. Right, I want you to get on with your work right now. No more talking, thanks.
Alice: Okay then.

Alice turns back, but continues chatting.

Teacher: Oh Alice?
Alice: Yeah?
Teacher: Could you repeat what I just said? What was my instruction?
Alice: To get on with my work and stop talking.
Teacher: Good. I'm glad you understand. I'd be disappointed to have to give you a detention. [*Smiles to suggest this is a possibility.*]

8 Set targets and time limits

Learning works best when you have a clear objective – a specific target at which to aim. Targets help you to harness a natural sense of competition, perhaps against others but, more importantly, against our own previous best. Having a clear amount to achieve, within a set time frame, gives a sense of urgency and pace to learning. It gives a clear structure – something definite towards which learners can work. Targets also help your lower-attaining children to feel a sense of achievement. If the teacher asks the class to work in groups to find five ideas in three minutes, even those who have the most difficulty should be able to contribute to this task.

You might use a whole range of different targets: a target for how many words or answers the learners must complete; a time for completing the activity; a target for improving behaviour, such as staying in seats. When setting targets, use the following tips to help you get it right:

- Make sure your targets suit the learners: don't make them too hard to achieve, nor conversely too easy.

- Keep targets short and specific for maximum impact – five words, three minutes, and so on.

- Add visual prompts to aid understanding, for instance, holding up five fingers to show 'five words'.

- Use your voice, or some music, to create a sense of pace and urgency. Try the theme tune from *Mission Impossible* or the conundrum music from *Countdown*.

- Use specific vocabulary to enhance your learners' motivation: words such as 'competition', 'prize' and 'challenge'.

- Make sure any rewards offered for completion of targets are ones that will appeal to the group or the individual.

To illustrate, here are some examples.

A whole-group target for behaviour – early years

'Right, children, I've got a very special challenge for you today. I want everyone to follow our golden rule – walk, don't run. Who thinks they can show me how we do this?'

An individual target for learning – upper primary

'Okay, Arwel. What I want you to do today is to concentrate on putting full stops in your writing, but they must be in the right places. Don't worry too much about spelling, because today we're going to focus on the punctuation. And if you do manage to put all the full stops in, I'll be able to give you a praise comment in your book.'

A whole-class target for learning – lower secondary

'Right. Today we're going to have a competition. As you can see, I've written ten questions up on the board about the learning we did last lesson. The first person to answer all ten, in full sentences, can leave first when the bell goes. Ready, steady, go!'

An individual target for behaviour – further education

'Could I have a quick word, Chris? Look, I know we've not been getting on that well, but I was hoping you'd do something for me today? The college has told me that I've got to fill out one of these yellow slips if I hear anyone swearing in our lesson. Could you help me keep an ear out for any bad language? Obviously, I don't want to have to fill one out for you, so your challenge today is not to say a single swear word. Do you think you can give that a go?'

9 Use humour

Humour is incredibly powerful in the classroom. Teachers who make their learners laugh, and who can laugh with them when appropriate, form good relationships with their classes. Of course, there are times when you can't see the funny side. On a Monday morning/Friday afternoon, when you're tired, hungover, coming down with a cold or are just plain cranky, you might not feel in the mood for a stand-up comedy routine. But if you can take a fun approach to the job, and make lessons feel relaxed and fun, this will help you to manage behaviour. Alongside its beneficial effects on your learners, humour:

- offers a respite from the tension that can build up with a difficult class
- makes learning fun for you and your learners

- helps everyone stay relaxed and rational
- helps you avoid defensiveness.

Use humour to dissipate low-level insults: be clear that you refuse to take this kind of stuff seriously and hopefully your learners will soon give up on doing it. With older learners, you can turn an insult on its head by agreeing with what the young person has said. So, if a learner says, 'Your hair looks really stupid like that', you might answer (deadpan), 'Yes, I know, and I'm planning to sue my hairdresser'.

Learn to laugh at yourself when you make a mistake, for instance, tripping over or saying something daft. Learners love a teacher who is willing to be self-deprecating. It's a good way of undermining the image of teacher as authoritarian figure, and it shows that you don't take yourself too seriously.

Generally, it is best to avoid sarcasm, although I appreciate it offers a way of letting off steam in stressful situations. Avoid laughing at individual learners or encouraging others to do so. Your 'class clowns' might enjoy the attention, but some shy children may be mortified if their peers laugh at them.

10 Put yourself in their shoes

When you're dealing with persistently difficult behaviour, it is easy to lose your sense of perspective. You begin to feel that learners are deliberately being awkward, and suspect that they have a personal vendetta against you. In turn, this can lead to overreactions to what are relatively minor issues. Develop the ability to step outside yourself, and to view what happens from your learners' perspective. Become a reflective teacher, constantly engaged in a process of self-analysis.

When an activity doesn't seem to be working, or the learners start behaving inappropriately, put yourself in their shoes to try to work out why:

- Is there too much listening and not enough doing?
- Is the concept too hard for the class to grasp?
- Do the learners find this particular topic boring?
- Is this work too easy for the group?

Sometimes you can't do much about the situation – the learners must get through a particularly tough or dull bit of learning. But if you put yourself in their shoes, you can understand why they might struggle. You can also analyse your own teaching by using this approach. If your learners often become confrontational with you when you try to discipline them, step back and view the way that you deal with behaviour from the outside. Are you saying or doing something to exacerbate the situation? Are there external factors at work?

When you take on the adult role of 'teacher', make sure you don't lose sight of what it was like to be a young learner. Sometimes people mess around because it's human nature to do so. Winding up your teacher has been a classic childhood pursuit, ever since schools were first invented. When I run training sessions for teachers, I find that even adults are sometimes tempted to muck around!

Part Two

The Teacher and Teaching

Chapter 4
The Effective Teacher

A learning process

Becoming an effective teacher is a learning process that starts the first time you set foot in a classroom, and is one that should never end, no matter how many years of experience you have. There are many different facets to being an effective teacher – skilled verbal and non-verbal communication, the ability to manage the class and the classroom space, an understanding of how to match teaching style to a particular situation, the knowledge to plan for and teach high-quality lessons. All of these qualities can be learnt and developed, and each of us will benefit from working on particular areas of our own practice. In this chapter, I look at those aspects of effective teaching that are connected to the teacher as a person and a communicator, rather than as an educator. (See Chapter 7, 'Effective planning and teaching' on page 93 for advice on planning and teaching the curriculum.)

It's probably fair to say that some people are born teachers – they have a natural ability to engage with and inspire others, to transmit ideas or knowledge, and to control the behaviour of groups of people. To an extent, this is about charisma, self-confidence and the power of personality. For these natural teachers, the skills and attitudes described in this chapter come instinctively. But we can't all be born teachers, and in any case, it's the willingness to learn and develop that is important, and not the point from which you start that process.

The teacher as role model

At first, the idea of being a role model takes a bit of getting used to. Sometimes you are a role model simply by virtue of your age, gender, subject area or social/cultural background. You might be the only male teacher working in your primary school, or the only female physics teacher in your local area. But the teacher as role model is about much more than this. It's about offering a consistent model of appropriate behaviour and attitudes, often for learners who lack this outside of an educational environment. Some of our most difficult learners are used to adults behaving aggressively: it takes time for them to realise that there are other ways of interacting with the world.

Young people model what they see, and it is worth keeping this in mind when you are frustrated by the behaviour of some of your learners (of whatever age). If a child is brought up in a house where every other word is a swear word, it is likely they will bring this language into school. When they come to respect you, learners will want to emulate you. They might copy your behaviour and your ways of relating to people; they might study a subject you teach to A level and beyond, because you have inspired them to love it as much as you do.

One of the key ways we can model appropriate behaviour for our learners is to treat them as we would wish to be treated ourselves, i.e. politely and with respect. We might hope that being polite would be a straightforward strategy to adopt and maintain. However, when faced with the stress caused by persistent aggression or rudeness, it is all too easy to get sucked into a similar frame of mind. Before you know it, you are making rude comments and being sarcastic – something you would probably never do in your life outside of school. Irritation is often an entirely understandable response, but at the same time it's not helpful.

A relentlessly polite manner helps you to:

- defuse difficult situations
- set an example of appropriate behaviour
- show others that it is possible to stay calm when dealing with frustrating situations
- stay 'in the right' and make it clear that the aggressive young person is 'in the wrong'.

The scenarios that follow show the teacher offering two very different models of behaviour. In the first instance, notice how the comments very quickly become a 'tit-for-tat' battle of rudeness. In the second, watch the teacher staying relaxed and defusing the situation.

For example...

Reacting 'in kind'

Teacher: Jason, get on with your work and stop causing problems.
Jason: No, I won't. This work is stupid and your lessons are boring.
Teacher: No, Jason, your attitude is stupid, not the work.
Jason: Don't call me stupid, you old cow.
Teacher: How dare you call me an old cow! Right, you're in detention.

Jason:	Oh yeah? Well I'm not coming to it. I hate you.
Teacher:	And I hate you too. [*Shouting*] NOW GET ON WITH THE WORK!

Modelling polite behaviour

Teacher:	Jason, I need you to get on with your work now, thanks.
Jason:	No, I won't. This work is stupid and your lessons are boring!
Teacher:	I'm sorry you feel that way. I do try to make them as interesting as possible. Now please get on with the work.
Jason:	No I won't! You're an old cow!
Teacher:	That's rather harsh. I'm not that old, am I, Jason? I'm not even 30 yet.
Jason:	[*totally confused by this response*] Huh?
Teacher:	Now please get on with the work. You have ten minutes to finish. I'd love to see how well you can do.

Unconditional positive regard

One of the keys to helping children and young people change their behaviour long term is to model the concept of 'unconditional positive regard' for them. This means helping them to understand that their behaviour does not define them – that you are able to see the person as separate from their behaviour. In other words, 'I like you; I just don't like your behaviour'.

In order to understand that they have agency over themselves and their behaviours, people need to believe that they can actively control and indeed change their behaviour. The adult's role is to communicate the message of 'unconditional positive regard' – no matter how you behave, I will still like and care for you – there are no 'conditions' on my regard for you. Saying this is not to *excuse* poor behaviour – the behaviour is still inappropriate – it just helps us ensure that we do not send children the message that they have 'become' their behaviour.

In order to demonstrate unconditional positive regard, be careful how you frame your conversations about, and reactions to, difficult behaviours. Aim to send the message that, while you dislike the poor behaviour, you still like the person behind it. Use phrases such as 'when you behave like x, it is upsetting for people because y'. Avoid using words that suggest a judgement on the child's character or personality, such as 'silly' or 'lazy'.

Effective verbal and non-verbal communication

When you step in front of a class, you take on a role to communicate with your audience, just as an actor does when they walk out onto the stage. Your learners take their cues about how to behave at least partly from the way that you use your voice, your face and your body. When you communicate confidence and certainty, this helps you to manage the teacher/child relationship. If learners respect you, because you communicate that you are interested in them and want them to succeed, they are more likely to behave for you.

It is important to think carefully about the physical aspects of your teaching, particularly if you are not naturally a confident person. Remember that you don't have to feel confident inside; you just need to communicate a confident persona through the verbal and non-verbal signals you send. Right from the start, your learners will be examining your teacher persona (often subconsciously), to figure out how they need to behave for you. A great tip, especially for new teachers, is to imagine yourself putting on your 'teacher character' before you interact with your class.

Using your voice

The teacher's voice is a tool, an instrument that we must use every single day of our working lives. It is vital that we learn to take good care of our vocal instruments – we only have one and we cannot send it away to be repaired. Some teachers are trained in good vocal technique (although by no means all). However, it's easy to pick up bad habits along the way. Make sure that you:

- maintain good posture, particularly when speaking
- stand upright with your shoulders, neck and chin relaxed
- breathe properly and use your breath to produce vocal sounds
- use your diaphragm to speak, rather than your neck muscles
- keep well hydrated throughout the teaching day.

If you are unsure about good voice usage, or if you regularly lose your voice, ask for some quality vocal training. Any music, singing or drama teachers will be able to give you good advice on how to best use your voice.

Your voice and your learners

Your voice says a lot about you to your learners: it has a powerful impact on their perceptions of you. We all have our own vocal style or personality, which tells others a lot about us as individuals. Think for a moment about the voices of some high-profile figures: where a vocal sound irritates you, this makes you feel negative about the person; a calm, gentle or interesting speaking voice helps to create a positive feeling.

The sound of your voice gives people clues about how you are feeling. When faced with a stressful situation, our voices very easily betray our emotions, becoming louder, higher pitched or cracking under pressure. Your voice offers your learners a clear indication of your inner state, and they will respond to the signals given. The secret is for you to be in control: if you need to change the sound of your voice, this should be a conscious decision, rather than being done as a result of stress. You might *feel* angry or upset, but you can still *sound* calm and controlled.

While you won't completely change the way you speak between the normal world and the classroom, you should significantly adjust it to create that 'teacher character'. For instance, speaking with a more pronounced tonal quality, and with a slightly slower pace than sounds natural, helps to support the learners' understanding of what you say. Reflect on how best you can adapt your voice to manage learning and behaviour. High-quality verbal communication:

- helps you to develop good relationships with your learners
- allows you to teach in a more engaging way
- helps your learners to learn more effectively
- encourages them to behave better
- protects your voice and prevents it from getting damaged.

There are some key aspects of voice usage that you can adapt and develop to support better behaviour.

Volume

It is tricky for teachers to achieve and sustain the right volume levels. Although we want to talk in a relaxed way to our learners, the stresses and strains of the typical classroom situation mean this is hard to maintain. When you find the right balance in your volume levels, your learners see you demonstrating emotional self-control; it also helps you to teach in a way that best allows for understanding.

Shouting often indicates a loss of emotional control, and some older learners might even enjoy getting their teacher to lose their temper and shout. Uncontrolled volume is also damaging for your voice, and it rarely has any direct impact on inappropriate behaviour. It signals an 'old-school' approach that is out of sync with modern approaches to education. Remember, some learners (typically the quieter ones you want to encourage) will feel scared if you shout at them. That is not to say you should never raise your voice. If you normally talk with a low volume level, raising it slightly gives a powerful impact. Combine a raised volume with a sharp tone and you can send a strong message of disapproval with relatively little effort.

To get volume levels right, and to avoid the urge to shout:

- Remember – the quieter you are, the quieter your learners must be to hear you. Encourage them to listen by lowering your volume levels. Don't overdo it and whisper, though, as a forced whisper can hurt your voice.

- Aim for a conversational volume level: stay alert to the way your emotional state affects the sound of your voice.

- When you feel yourself getting wound up, pause for a few seconds to regain self-control before you continue to speak. Breathe deeply and deliberately lower your volume levels.

- Learn to 'throw' your voice like an actor to an audience. Imagine the sound as a physical entity – a stone, for example – and 'throw' it towards your class.

- However, resist the urge to thrust your chin forwards to try and project your voice, as this will squash your larynx and be counterproductive.

- Talking loudly can be a matter of habit and teachers quite often talk more loudly than they need to. Learn to listen to yourself, as though you are standing outside yourself, to check whether your volume level is appropriate.

- To bring down your volume, imagine turning down the sound on a phone or stereo. Lower the sound by about half – you'll be surprised how quietly you can talk and still be heard.

- Take acoustics into account. If you teach in different spaces, adapt volume levels as appropriate. The empty space in halls and gyms makes your voice echo; a crowded classroom muffles sound.

- When you talk to an individual about their behaviour, get close and speak quietly, so no one else can hear.

- When you raise your voice, make it a conscious decision. Aim to do it from a position of emotional control, rather than as an angry or instinctive reaction.

As you learn to retain self-control, this helps your vocal technique as well. The sound comes from breath pushed by the diaphragm muscles, rather than from tension in the throat. Above all else, it's very important to remember to breathe, as breath is the starting point for voice.

Tone

Tone is great for adding interest and excitement to your teaching. It helps you to engage your learners, because it gives them clues and cues about your emotional state. There are many subtle ways you can adapt and vary your teacher 'character' by using different tones. A range of tones helps you to signal a range of thoughts, feelings, reactions and responses to your learners. The more you use tone, the more you will use your face and body as you teach. A deadpan voice gives a feeling of disengagement and tends to create a flat or lifeless facial expression. An animated voice, full of tone, lights up the face and eyes and creates a sense of connection with your learners.

The younger the children you teach, the more tone you can and should put into your voice. For those whose first language is not English, an exaggerated tone with lots of emphasis and facial expressions really aids understanding. Use a lighter touch with older learners: as we get older we begin to interpret excessive tone as being patronising. However, you can still be slightly more tonal than might feel natural.

Some useful tones for managing and supporting behaviour include:

- **Wonder:** put a note of wonder and interest into your voice to help you engage a class. You can also use this tone when you are particularly pleased with someone's behaviour: 'Oh, I'm so pleased with how you did that'.

- **Excitement:** an excited tone helps you to give pace and energy to a subject or activity. It also helps you to motivate and inspire learners.

- **Curiosity:** a curious tone is great for encouraging learners to take an interest in their learning. Talking about aspects of the curriculum in a curious-sounding way will support motivation.

- **Deadly:** this is a tone that tells your learners you are not happy. It can helpfully be used alongside a 'deadly stare'. It is a cold, calculated sound, rather than one of anger. Use it with older learners if they really let you down.

- **Disappointed:** disappointment is one of the most valuable tones for dealing with inappropriate behaviour. Where the class or learner respects the teacher, the feeling that 'you've let the community down' is a powerful motivating force for improvement.

Pace

Pace is a fascinating, subtle area of voice usage: to ensure learners can process and understand what you are saying, slow your pace down until it feels almost too slow. Bear in mind that children process verbal information at a different rate to adults, particularly children who have processing difficulties or for whom English is not their first language. Adapt the pace you use according to the learners you are teaching. With young children, or those whose language skills are not well developed yet, speak slowly and clearly. With learners who are disengaged, you can 'gee them up' by sometimes using a fast or excited pace to grab their interest, but avoid using it when all the words you are saying need to be fully understood.

Use a range of different paces during a lesson to add interest to the learning. Think of words as being like chewing gum – you can stretch them out in your mouth, or shorten them with a quick chomp, as required. It's a question of balance: keep your learners engaged but ensure that everyone can understand what you are saying.

A slow pace can:

- calm a learner down

- relax a tense situation

- quieten a noisy or overexcited group

- help ensure understanding.

But it can also:

- lead to boredom

- make learners switch off

- be perceived as patronising

- make the teacher appear self-important.

A fast pace can:

- motivate a disengaged class

- perk up an unmotivated learner

- give a lesson energy and forward momentum

- add interest to a dull area of the curriculum.

But it can also:

- hamper understanding

- make some learners feel stressed

- make the teacher sound harassed

- be wearing on your voice.

Teacher talk

It is worth considering how much you should talk. Teachers are a bit notorious for loving the sound of their own voices, beyond the point at which learners are actually taking in information. I know that I am sometimes guilty of talking at my learners far too much and for too long. When you speak to a class for more than about five or ten minutes, it is likely that at least some of your learners will have phased out the sound of your voice, and are contemplating inappropriate behaviour. The current focus on 'delivering' curriculum knowledge means that the emphasis is on a highly teacher-led approach. You will need to make your own judgements about the most effective amount of teacher talk during lessons.

Listening to someone talk for longer periods is typically a fairly passive activity and it is surprisingly easy to zone out and then realise that you didn't actually process what was being said. Think about yourself as an adult learner, for instance, in a CPD session which lacks interactivity – how long can you actually focus on and make sense of verbal input alone? When you do need to talk for longer periods, for instance, to give a detailed explanation of something, find ways to keep it interactive. Incorporate diagrams, demonstrations, examples, interesting resources, and so on. Intersperse adult-led teacher talk sections of lessons with the requirement for learners to do something. For instance:

- make notes
- write and show answers on a mini whiteboard
- pick out key words
- draw diagrams
- look at a visual aid
- handle a resource
- answer questions
- give their ideas
- talk to a partner
- do some 'actions'
- help you perform a demonstration.

Using your body

Teachers use a whole host of non-verbal signals to impact on learner behaviour. You will use some of these signals consciously, to help you control your classes. But you will also give subconscious signals, for instance, betraying a lack of confidence or conveying a feeling of stress. The way our learners interpret these signals helps them to make decisions about how to behave. The secret is to become aware of the signals you send, and to stay in control of them as far as possible.

There are good reasons why non-verbal signals are valuable for putting your wishes across in the classroom:

- They send a confident message about your status and ability to control the class.
- They require little effort from you, and do not put a strain on your voice.
- You can use them with individuals, without alerting the rest of the class.

- They help you avoid giving an audience to any learners who might want to get their peers' attention.

- Over time, they become a kind of non-verbal 'shorthand' that you use to talk to your class.

Your entire body plays a part in communicating with your learners – from your face right down to your feet.

The eyes and eyebrows

Use your eyes and eyebrows to build relationships with your learners and to manage their behaviour:

- When you're addressing a class, keep your eyes moving around, checking that all the faces are looking back at you. (I call this 'CCTV' – scanning for problems.)

- If they're not listening, pause. Don't continue talking until you have everyone's attention. Let your pause signal your intentions.

- Maintain your scanning around the classroom while activities are taking place, to check who is on task and who might need support or is losing focus: offer help to those who need it and nip any inappropriate behaviour in the bud.

- Use your 'deadly stare' with older learners – a quick glance/glare that says 'don't push it'.

- Raise your eyebrows to express surprise or disapproval.

- If you can, raise a single eyebrow to say: 'Excuse me, exactly what do you think you're doing?'

- When a learner is making a verbal contribution, maintain eye contact to demonstrate your interest and attention. Combine this with moving slightly towards them, to signal a keen interest in what they are saying.

Learners quickly get used to seeing you use your eyes to give non-verbal signals. When a class is not paying attention, try taking away eye contact from the class and looking at the ceiling instead. Where the teacher normally makes constant eye contact, this removal clearly indicates 'I'm waiting'.

The face

Your learners spend a lot of time looking at your face. If they see it is constantly moving, smiling and relaxed, but always alert, then they will believe that you are in charge and that you can control the group as a whole. Your face betrays any tension or defensiveness you feel, so make a conscious effort to keep your expressions cool and calm.

I'm sceptical about the old saying, 'Don't smile until Christmas.' Consider it as a metaphor – yes, be firm for the first term or so, rather than relaxing on behaviour too early, but definitely do smile. This not only shows that you are enjoying your teaching and feel relaxed enough to show it, but it demonstrates that you like your class as well.

The hands

Our hands are incredibly expressive – we 'talk' with them to our learners as readily as we do with our voices. Use your hands as a natural part of the teaching process to engage the class and create a feeling of inclusiveness. Hand signals become part of your 'shorthand' – you can tell the learners what you want without needing to speak.

Early years

- Put a finger to your lips to indicate that you want the children to listen.
- Tug on your ear to show that the children need to listen now.

Primary

- Click your fingers or clap your hands to gain attention.
- Place your hand on the desk of a child who is behaving inappropriately.

Secondary

- Hold one hand out, palm outwards, to say 'stop!'
- Give a 'thumbs up' signal to show well done.

Further education

- Make a circular motion with your fingers as you elucidate a point.
- Hold one finger upwards in the air to say 'wait'.

The stance

The stance that you take with your body communicates a great deal to the class, as does your overall posture. When you stand tall and keep your body open and relaxed, this demonstrates a lack of fear or concern. You can also use different positions to indicate your wishes and feelings. For instance, standing with your arms folded when you are waiting to begin the lesson, to suggest that you will not start teaching until the class falls silent. Keeping an upright posture has the added bonus of improving your voice usage, and is good for your back, so make this a priority.

Actions and non-actions

Teachers need to develop a repertoire of different actions to 'talk' to their learners. Balance movement with a sense of stillness, especially when you need the class's attention. You might look pointedly at your watch, to indicate that a class is wasting (their own) time. You could write down a learner's name during an incident of inappropriate behaviour – this can make them stop to ask what you are writing and why. If you go and sit with one group who are ready to begin the lesson, quietly chatting to them about how frustrating it must be that their peers refuse to fall silent, this communicates that you're going to focus on the learners who do the right thing.

Sometimes, if you refuse to take any action, you send as powerful a non-verbal signal as when you do something. For instance, you can call the class's bluff by waiting for silence, refusing to start teaching until the learners cooperate. Or literally 'freeze' like a statue to surprise your class into listening.

Levels

When a teacher always stands upright, above their learners, they communicate a subtle message of assumed superiority. Although you want to be in control of the situation, this does not mean you want your learners to believe that you see yourself as more important than them. By varying your body levels, you:

- show your learners that you are confident in your ability to keep control
- show that you respect them enough to come down to their level, literally and metaphorically
- lessen any perceived sense of authority or intimidation
- communicate much more effectively on a one-to-one basis
- keep your interactions private.

Sitting on the floor can work well, particularly with young children. Sitting on your desk creates an interesting shift in perspective too.

The teacher within the space

The way you use your teaching space communicates a complex non-verbal message about your style, and your levels of control. When we feel defensive, we might back into a corner, a place of safety. But unless you've used a seating plan, the rebels will be formulating their plans for revolution at the back of the classroom. And if you're stuck at the front, you won't be able to tackle them.

Teaching is a *physical* as well as an intellectual occupation, so get yourself moving around the room. Aim to:

- **Stand proud:** no matter how bad you are feeling, try not to let your body show it. Even if the class seems out of control, stand up proud, and give off an air of confidence.

- **Mark your territory:** move around the teaching space, prowling it a bit like a cat. Do this when the learners are busy with an activity, and while you are explaining the lesson. This helps to 'mark' the space as yours.

- **Surprise them:** keep your learners on their toes – make sure they never know when you might be approaching from behind. This is not to make them feel uncomfortable, but just to maintain a focus on learning.

- **Visit everyone:** aim to 'visit' all your learners during each lesson. Watch out for our natural tendency to focus on one side of the room more than the other (typically our dominant side, i.e. the left if you are left-handed and vice versa if you are right-handed.) Take care that you don't direct more of your teaching to one side of the room than the other. Aim to spread your attention and focus evenly around the space.

- **Use all the space:** stand at the back, the side, in the doorway – see your room from a range of perspectives. Sit in the learners' seats before a lesson too, so you understand how the room appears to them.

- **Get close to the characters:** move in close whenever you spot trouble brewing. Your presence will hopefully stop any issues before they arise. There is normally no need to say anything – learners quickly become uncomfortable about messing around when a teacher is standing close to them.

- **Surprise them!** Sometimes it is useful to suddenly change the spatial aspects of your style or your teaching space. You might rearrange the room from groups of desks to rows; clear the desks away and ask the class to sit on the floor; or even turn all the desks round to face in another direction. When you rearrange your space, this helps the learners to take a fresh perspective on what will happen in the room.

Psychological aspects of teaching

You can also use various psychological approaches to help you manage behaviour. It's as much about keeping yourself in a positive frame of mind as it is about keeping control of your class. Ideally, you want to feel calm, relaxed and alert. Try these ideas:

- **Keep them guessing:** although consistency is important, it doesn't pay to be too predictable all the time. Sometimes (and do it sparingly), make a sudden change in your teaching style. Perhaps you are normally quiet and firm. Once in a while, show the class that you have another, louder and sharper side to you.

- **Turn on a penny:** sometimes you can make a sudden change in your manner if it is necessary. For instance, you are having a really good lesson, when Matthew decides to spoil things by messing around. Turn to him, say, 'How dare you spoil this lesson for my wonderful class!' and then become 'sweetness and light' again instantly.

- **Convince yourself:** if you can convince yourself, really convince yourself, that you are in charge, then you will help yourself appear so. Know where you're coming from (be aware) and exactly what you want (be definite).

- **Maintain a psychological distance:** although it is hard, keep an emotional distance from the inappropriate behaviour that you encounter at work. Refuse to get emotionally involved with incidents of poor behaviour: this will help you to retain a sense of distance and a feeling of control.

- **Don't take it personally:** instead of seeing difficult behaviour as an attack on you, it is more effective to take a sympathetic view. Learners who behave inappropriately generally have problems of their own that at least partly cause the behaviour. No matter how difficult your class is, it is not the end of the world if some learners muck around, so don't let yourself view it in that way.

Chapter 5
Teaching Styles

What is a teaching style?

There are as many styles of teaching as there are teachers, because we are all individuals who work in unique ways. Lots of facets go together to make up a teaching style: your personality, the way you look, the way you speak, the way you use movement and space, the levels of control you use; everything you do in the classroom (and beyond) adds to your personal teaching style.

Each teacher's style is developed over the course of time. When you first start out in the classroom, you may be uncertain and lack confidence. You need a chance to experiment, to make mistakes and to find your feet. Remember, you won't be exactly the same person as a teacher, that you are outside the classroom. You can put on a confident teacher 'character', even if you feel shy and insecure inside. Being a teacher is as much about a class's perception of you, as it is about the reality of how you feel.

Whatever style you use, there are certain aspects and approaches that will help you best manage your learners' behaviour. Make a conscious decision to incorporate these strategies into your style, to help you control your learners' behaviour. An effective teaching style lets your class know that you are in charge, but in a positive, respectful and humanitarian way.

Different types of teaching style

Teaching styles fall somewhere along a line between passive, assertive and aggressive, with an assertive style being the ideal approach for effective behaviour management. If you understand the elements of these different approaches, you can achieve the right balance in your own teaching. Some of us lean naturally towards a more authoritarian teaching style, and need to curb our instinctive tendency to get wound up or overreact. Others tend towards a passive, defensive approach, and need to build confidence, self-assurance and self-belief.

Consider where you fall on the following spectrum:

Passive	Assertive	Aggressive

The conditions in which you work have an impact on the style you adopt. If you face lots of inappropriate behaviour, you can feel 'under attack' from the learners and tend to 'fight back' by becoming more reactive. But the more challenging the learners, the more likely they are to react badly to an 'attacking' teaching style. In an 'easy' school (if there is such a thing), you might tend towards over-passivity, allowing the learners to take control. Ironically, in an 'easy' school you probably need to add a bit of fire to your style.

Let's look in more detail at the three points on the spectrum.

A passive style

A passive teaching style is characterised by inactivity – the teacher stays 'inside' themselves, and is introverted and inward-looking, reacting to inappropriate behaviour rather than trying to proactively get in front of it. Other elements of a passive style include:

- The teacher uses a quiet voice and defensive postures.
- The learners control the classroom, rather than the teacher.
- The teacher uses more questions than statements.
- The learners are unsure what the teacher wants.

Here's an example of a passive teacher:

For example...

Rina is holding a paper aeroplane. She's disrupting the lesson by threatening to throw it across the room.

Teacher: Rina, what are you doing with that?
Rina: Nothing.
Teacher: Are you sure you're not doing anything?
Rina: Of course I'm sure. [*She throws the plane. The rest of the learners start making their own planes.*]
Teacher: But you said you weren't doing anything!

An aggressive style

With an aggressive teaching style, the teacher tends to come out of themselves and at the learners, 'attacking back' by being quick to judge and quick to lose their temper. Other elements of an aggressive style might include:

- The teacher overreacts to relatively minor inappropriate behaviours.
- There are clearly defined standards, but these are overly stringent.
- The teacher is never flexible when handling behaviour, regardless of the learner's context.
- The teacher's body language is hostile and they have a tendency to speak loudly and sometimes to shout.
- There is the potential for serious confrontation if a young person decides to take the teacher on.

Here's an example of an aggressive teacher:

For example...

Rina is holding a paper aeroplane. She's disrupting the lesson by threatening to throw it across the room.

Teacher: [*shouting*] What on earth do you think you're doing? Give me that right now!

Rina: But Miss, I was only…

Teacher: Don't give me that rubbish. Are you stupid or something? Aeroplane. Give it to me. Now.

Rina: Don't shout at me.

Teacher: Don't tell me what to do.

Rina: I'm not staying in your stupid lesson.

Teacher: How dare you call my lesson stupid!

Rina: I'm out of here. [*She storms out.*]

Teacher: Where the hell do you think you're going?! You're in serious trouble now…

An assertive style

With an assertive teaching style, the teacher asserts control of the situation while at the same time remaining reasonable and polite with their requests. They are proactive in getting positive behaviour from their learners, and explicit but not forceful about what this looks like. Other elements of an assertive style include:

- The teacher has clear, consistent and realistic expectations about behaviour and learning.
- The teacher is sure that the learners can live up to their expectations.
- The teacher is flexible when the situation merits.
- The teacher's body language and voice usage are relaxed yet confident.
- The teacher stays calm and polite at all times, treating the learners as they would wish to be treated.

Here's an example of an assertive teacher:

For example...

Rina is holding a paper aeroplane. She's disrupting the lesson by threatening to throw it across the room.

Teacher: Rina, I want you to give me that paper aeroplane right now, thanks.
Rina: No.
Teacher: Rina, I need you to give me the paper aeroplane right now.
Rina: But it's mine.
Teacher: Rina, if you continue to argue you will force me to put you in detention. [*Holds out hand and speaks calmly but very firmly.*] Give the paper aeroplane to me *now*.

Rina hands the paper aeroplane to the teacher.

In the day-to-day realities of the classroom, it is likely that your style will bob around on the spectrum between the different points. This is partly to do with your personality and how you as a human being feel on any particular day of the week. In addition, you'll be responding to the class, or to individuals within it. The more consistent a style you achieve, the more secure your learners will feel. With experience, you learn to achieve a consistently assertive style – proactive, interactive but with a strong sense of clarity, confidence and purpose. In the meantime, a great rule of thumb is: 'Ask once nicely, once firmly, then get on with it'.

Effective teaching styles

At its heart, the teaching style you use is a product of your personality. There's no point trying to copy those strict teachers at your school if you're shy, have a quiet voice and hate conflict. When we begin teaching, our style often mirrors our normal personality. With experience, we hone our style so that we present those aspects of ourselves that will work best in a classroom environment. We might temper our natural tendency to get overexcited, or work on our normal inclination to talk too slowly.

The style you use also needs to vary according to the age of the learners you work with, and the kind of environment in which you teach. Here are some different styles that I've seen over the years (I look at the first three commonly used styles in detail further below):

- strict and scary
- firm but fair
- comic and quirky
- earth mother/father
- brisk and business-like
- engaging eccentric
- drama queen/king
- one of the lads
- one of the kids
- close to the edge.

(This last one is often my own preferred style: the learners never know quite where you're coming from, and are fascinated to see what you're going to do next.)

Some teachers refine their style to perfection – their reputation as a 'type' of teacher is known around the school. (As in 'Watch out for Ms Davies; she's really strict and scary'.) You can also mix and match styles as appropriate. In a secondary school, you might be a bit more 'strict and scary' with your Year 7 form group, and 'one of the lads' when you teach Year 11 PE. Similarly in a primary school, you might be 'firm but fair' most of the time, but allow your more eccentric side out for some 'comic and quirky' art or drama activities.

The 'strict and scary' teacher

Most of us know a strict and scary teacher: maybe you work with one; perhaps you were taught by one when you were at school. The strict and scary teacher:

- demands perfect behaviour at all times
- has a high level of control over the learners
- loves to line a class up
- feels that working in complete silence is crucial
- sets the rules with no room for negotiation
- will often shout when applying a consequence
- uses more consequences than rewards.

Advantages

✔ The learners learn that they must behave, or they will be in trouble.

✔ It becomes progressively easier to discipline them, once they understand the tight boundaries.

✔ The class is well disciplined, and a good deal of work takes place.

✔ There is less likely to be disruption for attentive learners from peers.

✔ The teacher does not have to strive to be in a good mood all the time.

✔ They can relieve some of the stress by shouting at the class.

Disadvantages

✗ This style is physically tiring for the teacher.

✗ If there's a lot of shouting, the teacher's voice may suffer.

✗ The teacher needs to be physically imposing for this style to work, or have a strong 'presence'.

✗ Some of the quieter learners can end up in a state of fear.

✗ There is less opportunity for explorative, creative or group work, because the teacher wants to maintain silence and control.

✗ Although the learners behave for this type of teacher, they are unlikely to like them.

✗ There is more potential for serious confrontations to kick off.

The 'firm but fair' teacher

These days, you might hear the term 'warm strict' to describe an assertive, proactive teaching style, but my preference is for 'firm but fair', because to me 'strict' has negative connotations from my own school days. The learners tend to like firm but fair teachers and at the same time they also tend to respect them. Many teachers aspire to this style: it is the 'ideal' one in many situations. The firm but fair teacher:

- is clear with learners about the behaviour they expect
- sticks to the rules consistently
- applies some flexibility where appropriate – they flex the approaches, but not the standards
- raises their voice if needed, but only on rare occasions
- uses interesting activities and sets hard but achievable targets
- focuses on positive methods of motivation
- uses more rewards than consequences
- gets to know the learners as individuals.

Advantages

- ✔ The learners learn to behave through the application of consistent boundaries.
- ✔ Once they understand where the boundaries are, they follow them without having to be told.
- ✔ The class is well disciplined, and a good amount of learning takes place.
- ✔ This style is more relaxed, and less stressful for both teacher and learners.
- ✔ There is less chance of confrontations arising.
- ✔ There is more opportunity for creative, exploratory learning.

Disadvantages

- ✘ There's a fine balance to achieve between being 'fair' and becoming overly 'relaxed'.
- ✘ The teacher must be relentlessly consistent in applying the boundaries.
- ✘ This is tough when you're tired, stressed or overworked.
- ✘ The teacher needs to be in a good mood all of the time.
- ✘ Some learners may take advantage.

The 'comic and quirky' teacher

This is the style you often see in movies about teaching. It's the fun, inspirational, slightly eccentric teacher that I hope you had when you were at school, like I did. Although firm but fair is ideal, what's missing is that little bit of spice which makes the learners and the lessons come to life. The comic and quirky teacher:

- makes the lessons interesting
- hopes the learners might forget to behave inappropriately because they're enjoying themselves
- is keen for learners to love learning, love lessons and love subjects
- is good at being flexible when needed
- is not so good at being consistent, because they see this as less important than good relationships
- uses lots of tone and is not afraid to make a fool of themselves
- has a tendency to stand on furniture
- is popular with the learners.

Advantages

- ✔ The learners have fun – an often underrated quality in education.
- ✔ The learners do sometimes 'forget' to misbehave.
- ✔ Learning takes precedence over management/control.
- ✔ This style is very relaxed; there's less stress for the teacher.
- ✔ There is limited chance of confrontations arising.
- ✔ There are loads of opportunities for exploratory learning, with lots of creative thinking going on.

Disadvantages

- ✘ This style does not tend to be so popular with senior leadership.
- ✘ There's a balance to achieve between being 'fun' and 'focused'.
- ✘ Some of the experiments will go wrong.
- ✘ The class will often be one of the noisiest.
- ✘ Some quieter learners can feel overwhelmed by this style.
- ✘ This teacher isn't always great at dealing with quiet individuals.
- ✘ Some learners don't respond well to a humorous style, and might take some of the teacher's jokes in the wrong way.

Enhancing your teaching style

You can incorporate many subtle variations into your teaching style. Experiment with different approaches to see what works best for your learners and for you. Here are some suggestions for refining and enhancing your teaching style.

Buck the trend

Learners are quick to stereotype the kind of style they expect from you, depending on the way you look. If you're a physically imposing, rugby-playing kind of person, they may expect a 'strict and scary' approach. Buck the stereotype and challenge their perceptions by using a quiet but firm approach.

Be a real person

It's a tricky balance between being a teacher and letting the learners know that you are a human being as well. Being self-deprecating works very well in achieving the 'real person' effect. When you make a mistake, be willing to admit it. Be brave enough to laugh at yourself if you say something stupid. Don't be afraid to make a fool of yourself.

Don't try and be friends

Many new teachers make the mistake of being overly friendly with their learners, in the hope of keeping them on side. This is particularly tempting if you are close in age to them. Remember, though, this makes it hard to crack down on any boundary testing. Stay one step removed from your learners, no matter how well you get on with them.

Retain a 'mystique'

Although you want your learners to see you as a real person, it is not a good idea to give away too much of yourself. Teaching is not your entire life: it's psychologically beneficial to keep part of yourself separate from your work. Make it plain that you have a full and interesting private life, but one that you wish to keep mostly to yourself, thanks. You can occasionally let slip an amusing or thrilling anecdote, but do it sparingly.

Create a reputation

It's great when you overhear learners talking positively about your lessons with their peers. Word of mouth about a teacher has a huge impact on behaviour (for good or for bad). Remember, our learners discuss us outside of class, just as we discuss them. To build a good reputation you might:

- **Stay in the same place for a while:** as time goes by, your reputation (good, I hope) will precede you. Often, you'll teach younger brothers and sisters of learners you've already taught. And, I guarantee, they've discussed you at home before they arrive.

- **Use an unusual activity or lesson:** an inspiring activity influences your learners' behaviour; it also helps you earn an interesting reputation. See Chapter 7 for some examples of unusual starters and activities.

- **Make learning fun, sometimes:** when learners view you as an entertaining, fun, interesting teacher, they tell their peers about you. When these learners come to you, at some future point, they already have positive expectations of what you will be like.

- **Get involved:** interact with the learners outside of the classroom environment. Smile and say hello in the corridor; if your personal circumstances allow, get involved with extracurricular activities, like supporting a school football team.

Maintaining a positive approach

Teaching is not just about dealing with learners who behave inappropriately; it is also about working with those who always behave well. When you have to focus on dealing with difficult learners this can slant your sense of perspective. Pay attention to the learners who are doing what you want, and this will help you to get the critical mass on side.

With a positive approach, you retain your sense of humour and perspective, and you are far less likely to get stressed when things go wrong. You have a choice: see what happens in a positive light, or let it make you cynical and bad tempered. If you work with learners whose behaviour is very difficult to handle, I know it's easy to slip into a negative approach. When learners are ignoring you, being defiant, shouting abuse, it is all too tempting to expect the worst. The tension builds up inside you, even before the lesson begins. But remember, it's never every single young person in a group who is behaving badly, no matter how much it feels like it might be. To maintain a positive outlook:

- **Focus on what's going well:** sometimes the best way to deal with a difficult individual is to totally ignore them. If the behaviour is not affecting the learning for the rest of the class, give yourself permission not to pay it any attention. Allow yourself to focus on the learners who are doing the right thing for a while. Show that behaving well is the way to get your energy and attention.

- **Focus on your achievements:** take a moment to consider all the things that you are achieving. Perhaps getting the learners to stay in their seats, or to listen when you want to address your class, actually represents a huge achievement.

- **Keep yourself fresh:** teaching is exhausting, especially at those times of year when there are lots of meetings, consultation evenings and other demands outside of school hours. Leave yourself time for a life outside school – this will help you to keep your style fresh and positive.

- **Don't get defensive:** it's easy to slip into a frame of mind where you see everything in the worst possible light. React from your head and not from your heart. Refuse to let incidents of inappropriate behaviour cloud your whole style.

- **Use positive language:** make a simple change in the type of language you use to achieve a positive atmosphere in your lessons. Greet your learners by saying, 'Great to see you! I'm really looking forward to the brilliant work you're going to do today.' With such a positive approach, even the most cynical or jaded will hopefully be tempted to live up to your expectations.

Chapter 6
Thinking about Motivation

Why use motivators?

Motivation is a hugely complex topic because human beings are complex and multi-faceted. What motivates one person will leave another entirely cold. However, there are some general principles around motivation that it is very useful for teachers to understand and incorporate into their classrooms. The very youngest children are typically well motivated to play and learn – their behaviour reflects their intrinsic enjoyment of their interactions with the world. The older children get, the more demands the education system makes of them, and the harder it can be for them to feel motivated to focus, learn and behave.

In adult life, generally speaking, we get rewarded when we do well, for instance, by a pay rise at work, and we receive a consequence when we break the rules, for instance, if we get caught speeding. With some motivators it's clear-cut: you turn up to work every day at least partly for the tangible reward of a salary; if you break the speed limit in your car and get caught, you receive a fine and points on your driving licence. However, even here there are complications, because some people are happy to work in lower-paid occupations, in return for a sense of vocation. Similarly, the police have recently started to use 'driver awareness' courses for drivers caught speeding, in order to try and change their behaviour in the longer term. Perhaps you feel the biggest reward for being a teacher is the chance to 'make a difference'; maybe you stick to the speed limit near schools because you feel it's the right thing to do.

The longer I work in education, the more I understand just how complex and subtle questions about motivation can be. Certainly, there are situations where the use of both rewards and consequences has the potential to do more harm than good, because it encourages learners to see learning as something they have to be persuaded to do using external motivators. However, I think most teachers would agree that they are a useful strategy in a toolbox of potential techniques. Indeed, they are used in every setting I've ever visited. In the setting that I currently help to run, even though we don't use any extrinsic rewards, we still make use of intrinsic motivators and personalised praise.

Rewards can be helpful because:

- ✔ They help us to encourage appropriate behaviour and hard work.
- ✔ They help us to motivate learners, particularly those who do not have the intrinsic motivation to work hard.
- ✔ They act as a 'marker' that learners are doing well.
- ✔ They encourage teachers to take positive approaches.
- ✔ They boost learners who have low self-esteem.

Remember: a reward doesn't have to be a material 'thing'. The best reward of all is often simply a smile, a kind word, or telling the children how pleased you are with them.

Consequences can be helpful because:

- ✔ They give us a way of getting our learners to stick to the boundaries we set.
- ✔ They clarify the rules and the choices for children – if you do A, the reward is B; if you do X, the consequence is Y.
- ✔ They help us to teach learners about social mores – the written and unwritten rules and moral codes that structure our society.
- ✔ They act as a way of identifying learners who might need additional support with their behaviour.

Remember: a consequence that works really well in one setting, or with a particular age group, might be little use in another. Remember too that quite often consequences don't actually seem to change behaviour – without reflection on what happened, or support for learners to develop their self-regulation skills, consequences tend to act more as a tool for managing inappropriate behaviour than as a way to improve them.

Some thoughts on rewards

We all respond better to the carrot than the stick – to being encouraged towards something good, rather than being pushed away from something bad. When you use rewards and consequences, aim for a ratio of about five to one in favour of positive motivators. Look at the class both as a group and as a set of individuals, and consider what will motivate them. For the whole group, you can use rewards that work via peer pressure. With individuals, you can differentiate the rewards you use to suit a particular learner.

Rewards and your learners

Some learners would work hard and behave even if you didn't give them specific rewards – they have 'intrinsic' or self-motivation. These learners can defer gratification – they can handle short-term discomfort (slogging through the 'boring bits' of a subject), because they understand the long-term benefits of education. This could be because they:

- are naturally well-motivated
- have an instinctive curiosity, and are fascinated by learning
- have been taught that education is valuable
- enjoy working hard and find achievement satisfying
- find learning easy relative to other learners
- have a family that pushes them to achieve
- want to be successful to escape a background of deprivation.

Other learners lack an inner drive and struggle to keep themselves motivated. Often these learners need a blend of rewards and reassurance, as a kind of marker that the teacher has noticed and acknowledged them. Extrinsic rewards, such as stickers, certificates, phone calls home, etc. can be useful. Effectively, you are trying to develop the intrinsic characteristics of a self-motivated learner, such as those listed above, for those who don't already have them.

Getting rewards to work

To make rewards work for you, adapt them to suit your situation. Although your setting will have a policy on using rewards, you can also get creative with your approaches. (With consequences, consistency of use is much more critical.) Some of the most useful rewards run close to the wind – decide how far you can or should go. This will depend on your own values and opinions, and also on what your school allows. For instance, to keep a difficult class focused, you might offer them a highly valued reward of their choice (listening to music, some sweets). Although this is not strictly allowed, sometimes it's a case of 'whatever works'.

The most effective motivators tend to have some or all of the following factors in common:

When you're using rewards, follow these tips to get the best results:

- **Rewards must be wanted:** it's pretty pointless to use rewards your learners don't want. For a reward to have meaning, it must be valued by the recipient – the learners must want to receive it. Sometimes, teachers are not helped by the rewards on offer in their school behaviour policy, which don't really fit the learners.

- **Don't bribe them, surprise them:** studies have shown that the most effective reward is one received unexpectedly. Rather than telling your learners 'if you do this, you get this', a surprise reward is given out of the blue for pleasing work or behaviour.

- **Make rewards age specific:** different rewards work best with different age groups. Typically, the older the learners, the more they enjoy rewards which have monetary value (vouchers, stationery). Sometimes, however, the opposite effect occurs: a group of 15-year-olds who love getting stickers. Rewards can be used in an ironic, humorous way, especially if you have formed that kind of slightly jokey relationship with your class.

- **Make them earn the rewards:** ensure that learners earn their rewards fully, rather than handing them out for any old bit of decent behaviour or work. The harder rewards are to earn, the more we tend to value them. Where rewards are overused by some staff, this can devalue the currency for the rest.

- **Fit the reward to the individual:** within a class, there will be some who are desperate to get stickers, others for whom a phone call home is the ultimate prize. Be specific with your rewards – tailor them to the individual as far as you can.

- **Rewards have a sell-by date:** a reward might work well at first, then gradually run out of steam as the learners get used to receiving it. Regularly refresh the rewards system you use – both as an individual teacher and as a setting.

- **Reward all your learners:** sometimes you might find yourself getting trapped into giving lots of rewards to your tricky learners, to keep them on side and to get them to cooperate. But don't overlook those who work hard all the time – they deserve to receive recognition for their efforts as well.

- **Sometimes rewards need to be private:** most of the time, rewards tend to given publicly. Some learners, however, won't want others to witness their success – the peer group pressure against working hard or behaving well is too great. If this is the situation in which you teach, share your positive thoughts in private, for instance, in the corridor after the lesson.

Types of reward

Reward systems tend to be very similar in different kinds of educational establishments. Typically, stickers, merits, certificates and home/school contacts prevail. Some schools are becoming more innovative with the rewards that they offer, and you will find some of these more unusual ideas below. At post-16 level, it's tricky to find meaningful rewards. Of course, the most valuable reward is free and easy to give – praise from a teacher who the learners respect and like (it's earning that respect in the first place that's the hard part).

Below are some thoughts about rewards that you can use with your learners. Most of these are applicable to any age group (I've suggested adaptations as appropriate).

Individual rewards

- **Merits/commendations:** with well-motivated learners, merit systems can work well. A useful 'add-on' to a merit system is to give the learners points for their merits. They can 'cash in' points for vouchers, etc.

- **Certificates:** many schools use some kind of certificate to reward appropriate behaviour or high-quality learning, and these are often presented at a whole-school assembly. Adapt this idea in creative ways – 'learner of the week', 'friend of the week', the class votes for a winner, and so on.

- **'Special' tasks:** learners, especially the younger ones, love being offered 'adult' tasks, and at the same time this is useful for the teacher. Tidying resources, handing out books, sorting the cupboard. 'You be the teacher' is a popular reward: the young person gets to teach the class for a little while.

- **Stickers:** in schools where I've worked, these have been effective from nursery right up to GCSE level and beyond. (At 16+ years, they become a sort of in-joke between learner and teacher.) You can get personalised stickers that include your name and/or subject. Think ahead about where you want learners to put their stickers: on a jumper, a shoe, an exercise book. I once taught a child who would put them on his face.

- **Phone calls home:** teachers often tend to revert to phone calls home as a consequence for inappropriate behaviour, but they are more effective as a reward. Catch a difficult learner on a good day, promise a phone call home if they behave well, and start to build a positive relationship. Before phoning, check first about your school system for home/school contacts.

- **Writing home:** to make sure that you reward everyone in your class, at the start of the year, hand every learner a postcard and ask them to write on their home address. Pop the pile in your drawer, and aim to fill out three or so each lesson. This helps ensure that eventually you find a reason for everyone to receive a postcard home. The great thing about a postcard, as opposed to a standardised letter, is that it can be stuck with a magnet on a fridge door, as a constant reminder of the teacher's approval.

- **Sweets and other treats:** when I first started teaching, no one would have raised an eyebrow if you gave sweets to your learners. These days, with a focus on healthy eating, it's a brave teacher who tries this approach. Suffice to say, these are a popular motivator and there's no need to make a big song and dance about it; just check for allergies and ensure that the treats you choose are halal and vegan friendly.

- **Raffles:** the teacher gives out raffle tickets for good work or behaviour, and then holds a draw at the end of the lesson or the week, with a prize given to the winner. Sometimes these raffles are held across the school, and for longer periods of time (e.g. a term), with really great prizes at the end.

Group rewards

Group rewards work well, because they utilise peer-group pressure. Encourage your learners to work together to achieve these rewards.

- **'Special' time:** the chance to earn privileges is a very effective reward – it shows the link between appropriate behaviour and positive consequences. The idea of a special (golden) time is widely used in primary classrooms: the learners earn (or lose) the right to free-choice time on a Friday. You can adapt this for older learners with five minutes' 'social time' at the end of lessons.

- **Music:** earning the 'right' to listen to music is popular with older learners. Put on the radio, or offer a selection of your own music, rather than allowing learners to bring in their own (this avoids any issues with inappropriate language).

- **Marbles in a jar:** the teacher has an empty jar on their desk; every time someone works hard or behaves well, a marble goes in the jar. When the jar is full, the class receives a treat (for instance, a picnic with takeaway pizza). Spice up this idea by putting different objects in the jar – crystals, Lego pieces, dinosaur 'droppings'.

- **Trips:** the chance to go on a trip is a powerful motivator. It has the added benefit of leaving a positive and beneficial 'afterglow' for those involved, and of course it's educationally valuable too. One drawback is that it does require a lot of work to organise this kind of event.

From extrinsic to intrinsic motivation

The ideal is for our learners to be intrinsically motivated to work hard and to behave. We want children to want to learn and behave because of an inner motivation, rather than because we offer them something in return for their compliance or cooperation. We want to send the message that it is the *learning* and not the reward that matters. Although it is typically simpler to offer a sticker, or a certificate, or a merit, these external rewards encourage children to behave because of what they hope to receive by doing so. Our aim should be to help them learn a more appropriate set of reasons for behaving.

Schools and teachers use a variety of methods to move children towards a more intrinsic set of motivations. You might:

- drop in regular rewards, to encourage your learners to reach personalised targets

- contact the family, to explain how to support the learner in achieving better behaviour

- be a positive role model, and someone who expects them to achieve great things

- make the learning rewarding, to build curiosity and the desire to learn for its own benefits

- build on your learners' interests, and be inventive in how you present the curriculum, to show them how it is possible to feel intrinsically motivated to learn even what seems like the driest of topics

- differentiate the learning and adapt your teaching to ensure that it is accessible to all

- offer practical support for those children who do not get it at home, for instance, running a breakfast club or homework session

- show your class the connection between education and work, for example, by organising work experience or by hosting a visit from a former pupil who has gone on to have a successful career.

Some thoughts on consequences

No one likes to be punished: giving a consequence has the potential to do damage to your relationships with your learners. So, when you do have to use consequences, you've got to get it right. Consider your own response to the threat of being punished. You're driving along the road when you see a speed camera. What do you do? (I'm assuming you check your speed and slow down if necessary.) And what makes you behave in that way? For the consequence to work, you need to be:

- aware of what the rules are in the first place
- aware of what the consequence is for breaking them
- fairly certain you will get caught if you break the rules
- sure that if you are caught, you will receive a consequence
- worried enough about the consequence to want to avoid getting it.

Exactly the same principles apply when you use consequences with your learners. If they know what the rules are, and they don't want the consequence they'll get for breaking them, you are halfway there.

The best approach when using consequences is to stick closely to your behaviour policy: consistent use of consequences is best for staff and fairest for learners. A great tip is to 'blame the policy' – your role when giving consequences is one of enforcer – you are applying the rules set by the organisation. Your main job is to teach, rather than to discipline, so you apply the policy as stated. Sometimes your policy will not serve you or your learners well, or will not include consequences that the learners wish to avoid. If that's the case, you'll need to duck and dive a bit to get things right. To make the most effective use of consequences:

- **Ensure that they're unwanted:** consequences must be something the learners want to avoid, or they won't act as an effective deterrent. This is a key problem with some of the 'zero tolerance' type systems that are popular in the current educational climate: if your learners don't care about getting detentions, then giving them can become counter-productive, and the same learners can basically end up missing most of their lessons.
- **Make sure they're proportionate:** if a teacher reacts to a minor offence by immediately throwing the learner out of class, this suggests that they've

been looking for an excuse to get rid of that person. Unless the inappropriate behaviour is really serious, start with the lowest level consequence.

- **Make them fit the 'crime':** the best consequences give both learner and teacher a sense that justice is being served. If a learner scribbles on a desk, the most fitting consequence would be to clean off the scribbles.

- **Consequences must be followed through:** when you give a consequence, it must be served, or it's pointless giving it in the first place. If it's not served, next time round your learners know that you make empty threats. With short detentions in a school where there is not a centralised system, this can mean chasing a learner endlessly to serve their time – it's a lot of hassle, but it really is worth doing.

- **Don't threaten what you can't or won't deliver:** when we are stressed, it is tempting to throw out threats about all the terrible things that will happen to the class if they don't stop messing around. Don't threaten something you have no intention of doing – it makes you look unreliable.

- **Avoid the threat of 'somebody else':** sometimes a teacher threatens to send a learner to 'somebody else' (typically a senior leader). Unfortunately, all this does is suggest that you cannot deal with the situation yourself. As a first step, aim to deal with behaviour problems yourself, only referring a learner to someone else if the issue really merits it.

- **Don't use whole-class consequences:** it is never everyone in a class who is behaving inappropriately, so using whole-class consequences will probably just annoy your most cooperative learners, who will feel unfairly treated.

- **Beware unintended consequences:** one of the biggest issues with giving play-time detentions is that the learner then doesn't have the chance for a break. Some young people end up in detention at break, lunch and after school. This can become a vicious cycle, in which they never have time to eat, play or socialise, which in turn impacts negatively on their behaviour in class.

- **Aim to include a restorative element:** the reason the police now use the option of driver awareness courses is that these have been shown to be more likely to change driver behaviour in the longer term. Where the consequence includes some kind of discussion about what happened, why it was a problem, and how they can avoid it happening again, this helps the learner understand how to change their behaviour. Talk about the impact of the behaviour on other learners and encourage them to see why it was inappropriate.

Types of consequences

There are many different consequences you can use to help you control behaviour. Remember that the most effective consequence is often the simplest – a disappointed look or a word about how unhappy you are – *provided the learners respect the teacher or want to please them in the first place.* (In some very challenging settings, the amount of difficult behaviour means that these low-level approaches have little impact.) Unless the behaviour is very serious, start with the most minimal form of intervention, and work up gradually.

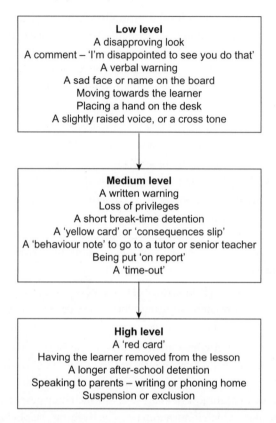

Low level
A disapproving look
A comment – 'I'm disappointed to see you do that'
A verbal warning
A sad face or name on the board
Moving towards the learner
Placing a hand on the desk
A slightly raised voice, or a cross tone

Medium level
A written warning
Loss of privileges
A short break-time detention
A 'yellow card' or 'consequences slip'
A 'behaviour note' to go to a tutor or senior teacher
Being put 'on report'
A 'time-out'

High level
A 'red card'
Having the learner removed from the lesson
A longer after-school detention
Speaking to parents – writing or phoning home
Suspension or exclusion

Something else worth trying is the 'comedy consequence', especially if you have a good, jokey relationship with a class. For instance, you might threaten to sing to them if they don't stop talking (assuming your singing voice is as awful as mine).

Detentions

In most secondary (and some primary) schools, detentions are one of the most frequently used consequences, so it's vital to get them right. Depending on your school situation, detentions may work very well, or they may be of practically no use at all. Many secondaries now use a centralised detention system, which alleviates some of the workload caused by having to chase learners to serve detentions. You will need to use your professional judgement to decide whether detentions are a helpful consequence in your context. Where you do use them:

- **Make sure they're served:** in a secondary school, chasing learners to serve detentions is often very time-consuming – that brief moment of inappropriate behaviour in class turns into a cat-and-mouse game of epic proportions. But if you chase the first few times, the learners soon realise that they might as well turn up. If you're not willing to chase up on missed detentions, you would be better off not using them at all.

- **Get them served quickly:** ideally, there should be a clear link between the inappropriate behaviour and the consequence, so get detentions served as quickly as possible. It is far better for learners to serve an initial short detention, than for you to have to refer them for more serious consequences.

- **Use a 'collection service':** in secondary schools, a major issue is when you need a learner to return to you at a break time or at the end of the day. If they fail to turn up, you must then chase them to serve the consequence. To avoid this, send someone reliable to go and fetch your detainee a few minutes before the bell goes (agree this with their teacher beforehand).

- **Think about what happens during detentions:** you might take the opportunity to have a chat about why the inappropriate behaviour happened, and what can be done to stop it happening again. You could devise a community consequence: collecting plates in the dining hall, or picking up rubbish. If the consequence is for work not done in class time, the learner should finish it in detention.

How to apply consequences

When you come to apply consequences, the way that you do this has an impact on how your learners react to them. Unless the situation is very serious, avoid confrontation by giving a series of warnings first.

With very young children, a distraction is often far more effective than a consequence. This can work well with older learners as well, particularly with those who are trapped in habitually inappropriate behaviour, and who need you to show them a way out.

The advice below covers both the behaviour management techniques you should use when giving consequences, and also some tips about your use of voice, body and space.

Behaviour management techniques

- **Defer if necessary:** don't feel that you always have to give a consequence immediately the inappropriate behaviour occurs. If you're trying to introduce the lesson and one child is being disruptive, you might say 'I'll talk to you about your behaviour in a moment', then go on to complete your introduction. Once the class is on task, you can deal with the child in relative privacy. A good rule of thumb is: 'Is this inappropriate behaviour immediately interfering with my ability to teach the class?' If not, you can defer.

- **Make the situation clear:** misunderstandings can lead to unnecessary confrontations, so always make your position crystal clear. State your expectations clearly, telling the learner exactly what you want, then clarify how the learner's behaviour is failing to meet your expectations.

- **Make your feelings clear:** learners who behave poorly often have issues with a lack of empathy. Explain how the behaviour makes you and the other learners feel, and how it impacts on the learning for the class. Encourage learners to see how others view their behaviour, and consequently why it is unacceptable.

- **Offer a positive alternative:** sometimes, learners back themselves into a corner when they behave inappropriately, and it is up to you to offer them a way out. Offer a volunteer task to complete, or suggest an alternative activity.

- **Disapprove of the behaviour, not the child:** remember, the problem is not the learner, but the learner's behaviour. Remember this to help you depersonalise consequences. 'When you talk over me, the class can't hear what I'm saying' as opposed to 'Sam, you're talking again – why are you always talking?' Your use of consequences is not a personal attack on the learner, but a logical and consistent response to their behaviour. Aim to send the message that you still care about the child despite their behaviour.

- **Use 'the choice':** this strategy, described in Chapter 3, helps you to depersonalise consequences, and throws the responsibility for the situation back on the learner. The choice is simple: 'Either you stop the behaviour now, or I will have to apply this particular consequence.'

Use of voice, body and space

- **Start with a check-in:** often, the best first step is a genuine question about the learning, such as, 'Is there something I can support you with, to get you started?' Keep the door open to the possibility that the learner just needs your help in settling to work.

- **Keep it private:** move beside the learner, or ask them to step to one side for a moment to talk with you. Use a quiet voice, so that the rest of the class can't hear. If you embarrass the learner in front of their peers, this ups the stakes and can lead to confrontation. Don't give your troublemakers the 'oxygen of publicity'.

- **Remember! Repetition is vital:** repeat a warning to ensure it has been heard. Say the learner's name several times to make sure they are listening. Don't assume something will be heard the first time you say it.

- **Tell, don't ask:** assert yourself by the use of positive commands, rather than using questions which suggest the behaviour is optional. Use 'I want', 'I need you to' and 'Let's see you' type statements, rather than 'Could you' or 'Will you'. Tell your learners exactly what you want them to do – they need to know.

- **Stay relaxed:** keep your responses calm and low-key. Before you speak, breathe deeply a few times to ensure you are rational rather than emotional. If possible, coax the learner into complying, rather than wading straight in with a consequence.

- **Be polite:** if a learner is rude and defiant, you may feel tempted to blow off steam by being rude yourself. Don't descend to the same level – remember, model the behaviour you want to see.

- **Use a tone of regret, rather than revenge:** aim to sound unhappy and disappointed that you have had to use a consequence. Don't let a vengeful tone creep into your voice, no matter how you feel inside.

Of course, when you give a consequnce you won't always be dealing with an individual – often several learners will be behaving inappropriately, all that the same time. When this happens, you could:

- highlight the learners who are doing as you wish – remember that golden ratio of 1 consequence to 5 rewards

- deal with the worst offender first, to make an example

- deal with the easiest person first, and hope the others notice

- use a completely non-verbal approach – look cross, then start to move towards the problem person

- grab a pile of behaviour slips and start to fill them out

- aim to distract everyone by making a sudden change in the lesson.

Here are two examples of a teacher applying a consequence, showing how the learner might react to different approaches.

For example...

A good way to apply consequences

Carly has arrived at her Year 9 science lesson in a very bad mood. She is wandering around the room, chatting to the other learners. The teacher is ready to take the register and wants to start the lesson.

Teacher: Carly, I need to get going with my lesson now. Could you hand out these exercise books for me while I take the register?
Carly: [*distracted by this*] Oh, okay.

Later in the lesson Carly gets up again and starts to wander around. The teacher motions her to one side to speak privately with her.

Teacher: Carly. We have a rule that we stay in our seats in science: it's really important for everyone's safety. I need you to sit down right now, thanks.
Carly: No I won't. I'm bored. This lesson is stupid.
Teacher: Well, Carly, I'm sorry that you feel that way. You have a choice. Sit down right now, get your work done and go on time. Or I'm afraid you will force me to give you a written warning.
Carly: That's not fair! I'm not doing anything wrong!
Teacher: Carly. I want you to sit down in your seat *right now* and get on with your work. Last chance. Don't push it.

At this stage Carly will either comply or the teacher will have to apply the consequence.

A bad way to apply consequences

Carly has arrived at her Year 9 science lesson in a very bad mood. She is wandering around the room, chatting to the other learners. The teacher is ready to take the register and wants to start the lesson.

Teacher: [*across the room*] Carly! Can you sit down please? I want to start my lesson.
Carly: Well, I don't want to start your lesson. Your lessons are boring.
Teacher: Don't be so rude! Look, why can't you just sit down and let me get on with taking the register?

The rest of the class are watching the confrontation with interest. Carly is now enjoying the 'publicity' of being reprimanded in front of the class.

Carly: No, I won't sit down. Are you gonna make me?

Teacher: Yes, I am going to make you. You're in an hour's detention with me after the lesson.

Carly: That's not fair! I'm not coming!

Teacher: Yes you are. Now shut up and sit down.

Carly: You can't tell me to shut up! I hate you and I hate your lessons. I'm out of here!

Carly storms out of the room.

Chapter 7
Teaching for Positive Behaviour

Teaching and behaviour

In teaching, there are lots of things that you can't change or have much of an impact on. You can't change the learners you work with; you can't change the background they come from or the local context; you can't change the way they've been brought up, or what their parents are like; you can't change the leaders who run your setting, school or college; even though you can improve the general look of your classroom, you can't get yourself moved to a different teaching space overnight; and you can't change the demands that come to you from the DfE or Ofsted.

But the biggest thing you can change, the place where you can have the most influence and also feel a sense of creativity and empowerment, is the way that you go about planning and teaching your lessons.

It's important to remember that the reason you need to manage behaviour in the first place is so that you can get on with teaching. That's what you're in the classroom for, after all. As part of your quest to get your learners behaving, you need to plan and teach high-quality lessons. Although this isn't a magic formula for getting perfect behaviour, it is one part of your practice that you can adapt very easily.

Think back to when you were at school. If you were in a lesson that was:

- fast-paced
- engaging
- interesting
- weird
- surprising
- disgusting
- exciting
- or funny

… I bet you and your peers were more likely to behave.

This is categorically not to say that every lesson can or should be an all-singing, all-dancing, multimedia extravaganza. There will be days when you are so tired that you can barely drag yourself into school; other times when the subject you're teaching is dry and hard to spice up. Nor is it to say that it is somehow the teacher's *fault* when learners behave inappropriately – it is their behaviour, not yours. But I think we would all admit that if we are in a poorly run INSET, or a boring meeting, we are more likely to behave inappropriately, even though we're good at keeping our poor behaviour 'under the radar'. If most of your lessons are interesting, and learners feel like they are learning effectively and being treated respectfully, then they will be more inclined to behave themselves for you. You'll also get yourself that all-important good reputation.

Of course, there's a balance to be struck between what learners view as interesting activities and what is educational. After all, given the choice, some might prefer to spend the time playing computer games, or be out on the football pitch. As their teacher, you must get through the curriculum and teach them the skills they need. Inevitably, it will be difficult to make some of the material you must teach stimulating, while still covering all subject areas. On the whole, though, learners forgive the occasional dull lesson from a teacher who normally teaches in a way that engages them.

At the moment, education (in England) is going through a time when the focus is very much on 'delivering knowledge'. All the messaging from both the DfE and Ofsted focuses on this, and it can be hard to push back against the tide. But bear in mind that these things go in cycles – I often say to new teachers that you need to hold tight to your values, and continue to demonstrate those values through your approach, because if you stick at it long enough, in ten years' time everyone will say that you were doing the right thing all along.

Before I describe how you might 'teach for positive behaviour', I'd like to deal with some of those things that could stop you from being experimental and creative. You could be worried about:

- getting through the curriculum
- what might happen if you give your trust to your learners
- the noise and mess that could be created
- whether the learners will get overexcited and go wild
- what other teachers, senior leaders or inspectors might think.

Let's deal with each of those concerns in turn:

'I'm worried about getting through the curriculum'

If your learners are behaving inappropriately, you can 'get through' it all you like: they probably won't learn it or remember it though. Don't be a teacher who just ticks the curriculum boxes; be a teacher who wants them to learn. Also, remember that behaviour is effectively part of your overall curriculum anyway, especially if you work in the early years, where it is explicitly referred to in the areas of learning.

'I'm worried what might happen if I give my trust to my learners'

The more often you trust them, the more likely they will be to honour that trust. My experience suggests that the more 'difficult' the learners, the better they actually respond to being given your trust.

'I'm worried about the noise and mess that could be created'

If the noise reflects engagement with the lesson, that's a good, not a bad, thing. And if it's mess that concerns you, get them to tidy up afterwards.

'I'm worried that my learners will get overexcited and go wild'

They might do, the first time you try something experimental. But when they do, you learn the techniques needed to pull back from that situation. And next time round, it won't be so hard.

'I'm worried what other teachers, senior leaders or inspectors will think'

Who are you doing this for? If the answer is 'my learners', then who cares what everyone else thinks? Be brave enough to use your own professional judgement, and refuse to care what others think when they don't know your learners as well as you do.

If you think back to your own schooldays, I hope that you too can remember one or more teachers who really inspired you, who filled you with a passion for learning or for a particular subject; who perhaps even inspired you to become a teacher yourself. Being in a position to inspire the next generation is an incredible honour – our influence lives on long after we do. Although teaching with passion, energy and enthusiasm is hard work at times, it has got to be worth it when you consider the potential benefits.

Effective planning and teaching

There is great skill involved in planning and teaching high-quality lessons. Learning how to do this takes time, but eventually you get a feel for what will be effective. With experience you also learn to adapt your teaching for different classes and different learners, eventually even during the lesson itself. Although workload is a huge issue in teaching, especially at the moment, planning lessons should be enjoyable: use your imagination, and think laterally about different ways of putting across a topic.

As a trainee or new teacher, you'll have to put lots of detail in your lesson-planning. Play the game and plan as your lecturers expect you to plan – a detailed plan helps you to think through your lessons in advance and gives you a sense of security. However, once you qualify and begin to experiment, you might find that too much prescriptive planning tends to work against good-quality lessons. Having too much detail in your plan can:

- tempt you to stick to something that isn't working
- mean you are stuck to your desk, referring to your notes, while inappropriate behaviour is plotted at the back of the room
- make you unresponsive to the mood of the class
- mean you lose the 'feel' that is needed to pace and time a lesson.

The ability to engage, interest and excite your learners depends on a whole range of different factors – the format and content of a lesson, and also the way it is delivered. Get these aspects right, and you stand a much better chance of encouraging positive behaviour.

The format of lessons

Lesson format is the 'nuts and bolts' of good planning – it means giving a clear and effective structure to class time. Generally speaking, learners want to have this structure to their learning, and it's particularly important for those learners who present you with behaviour issues. A good lesson format helps to keep your learners focused and on task. The strategies that follow will help you to format your lessons effectively.

'Mapping' the lesson

Teaching a lesson is a bit like setting out on a journey – the teacher knows what the destination is (the aims, objectives, success criteria), but the learners don't yet know where you're going. When you've spent ages planning a session, it's tempting to believe that the learners will somehow 'know' what it is going to be about, without any explanation. If you then launch straight into the subject, the learners get confused, feel a lack of clear structure and purpose, and are more likely to start messing around.

You can let your class know where the lesson is going by doing some or all of the following:

- explaining your aims
- talking about your objectives
- establishing the success criteria
- telling them your 'WALT' – 'we are learning to'
- letting them know your 'WILF' – 'what I'm looking for'
- writing an outline of the format up on your whiteboard
- explaining the timings of the session
- getting the learners to devise a set of questions they'd like answered.

However, not every single lesson has to have this tight, pre-ordained format (unless your school demands that it follows a specific structure, unfortunately something that is more common at the moment than it should be). Sometimes you can take a journey in a lesson without having an exact sense of where you're going to end up. You might bring in an inspirational resource, or ask the class a question, to get things going. At other times, a lesson may deviate entirely from its original intention ('destination'), because you realise pretty quickly that what you had planned just doesn't suit the learners.

Tasks and activities

Since a lesson is basically made up of a series of tasks or activities, the way that you format these will have a significant effect on your learners' behaviour. For the best results:

- **Keep the tasks short and focused:** the longer you spend on any one activity, the more chance there is for the learners to get bored and go off task. With lots of short, purposeful exercises, you create a strong sense of focus and pace.

- **Set clear targets:** be sure about what and how much you want your learners to achieve, whether it's five ideas or half a page. Reward the completion of each target before you move on to the next.

- **Set clear time limits:** similarly, be clear about how much time is available to complete the activity. If you give the learners 20 minutes, they may use half of it chatting before they begin, or half of it chatting after they've finished. If it looks like the learners are finishing early or need more time, stretch or condense the actual time to suit their needs.

- **Keep the pace up:** using short, focused tasks creates a sense of pace and forward momentum: this is useful in engaging learners with shorter attention spans.

- **Break up longer tasks:** where you need to set longer periods of time for activities, break the time up by getting the learners to stop and share ideas, or discuss what they've done so far.

- **Use a variety:** try a mix-and-match approach – ensure that there is plenty of variety in the tasks you do. This helps you appeal to different learners.

At the end of your lesson, talk with your learners about what they have achieved and use targeted, specific praise reward them for efforts. Create a sense of success, so that they are more likely to behave and work well the next time you see them. A plenary gives a good sense of completion to the lesson journey.

As well as devising activities yourself, get your learners involved. In the Foundation Stage, the children spend much of the time choosing the activities they want to access (although the resources you set out have an influence on what they learn). With older learners, the teacher tends to have more say in the activities they do. Instead of always being the one holding the reins, hand over the lesson journey to your learners from time to time.

The content of lessons

Planning and delivering the content of a lesson should be where the fun lies. Our role is to get ideas, facts, skills and information across so that our learners can learn them. When you make a subject accessible, this gives you a sense of achievement; it also helps to keep your learners on task and hopefully behaving themselves. Engaging lesson content could include some or all of the following elements:

- Make it enjoyable.
- Make it relatable to real life.
- Make it multisensory.
- Make it topical and relevant.
- Use interesting props and/or resources.
- Make it big, colourful and eye-catching.

Let's deal with each of these in turn.

Make it enjoyable

This involves lateral thinking. Learners tend to see lessons as enjoyable if they feel as little like work as possible: it's a bit like hiding vegetables in a pasta sauce as a parent – hide the learning behind the fun. You could try:

- a crime scene (see 'The scene of the crime' on page 102)
- a quiz
- activities with formats based on a TV show (*Great British Bake-Off, I'm a Celebrity, Get Me Out of Here!*)
- educational games.

Make it relatable to real life

Those learners whose behaviour proves most difficult to manage are often the learners who fail to see the link between education and the real world beyond. Bring this alive for them by creating real-life scenarios in your classroom. For instance, with younger learners you could:

- Work as 'spies' to find clues and use different mark-making methods.
- Become 'builders' to make a wall with bricks, sand and water.
- Act as circus performers to practise balancing, juggling and tumbling.

Make it multisensory

In a typical lesson, learners use only a limited palette of senses – often just their sight and hearing. Incorporate activities that involve as many of the senses as possible. Your learners could touch objects, smell plants, taste foods. Be creative, whatever the curriculum area:

- In maths, sort spices (cardamom pods, star anise) rather than blocks.
- In geography, go on a sensory walk around the local area.
- In art, make 'smelly sculptures' by adding food flavourings to playdough or clay.

Make it topical and relevant

Show how the learning relates to current events, or to the learners' interests. Demonstrate that education is a fundamental part of, and not separate from, the world beyond school. For instance, you could link big sports events (the Football World Cup, the Olympics) to learning in:

- numeracy/maths – scoring, trajectory, stadium capacity
- geography – flags and anthems from around the world
- literacy/English – poems about scoring a winning goal, writing publicity materials and programmes.

Use interesting props and/or resources

Learners of all ages love getting their hands on *things*, especially things that aren't normally found in a classroom. Be creative – go for the unusual to catch their attention. Have a think – what could you do in your subject/ age range with:

- a pack of cards
- a toilet seat

- a sheep's skull
- a lottery ticket?

When it comes to using objects, anything that makes your learners go 'urrgghhh!' will work very well – a steaming pile of horse droppings, a weird-looking bug you found in your garden.

Make it big, colourful and eye-catching

To catch your learners' attention, have fun playing around with size and colour. You could try:

- using giant, oversized objects
- adding vivid colours to a presentation
- drawing a giant picture with chalks on the ground outside
- using a simple two-tone effect of black and white for a display.

Anything that catches the eye will draw your learners' focus and hopefully (even if only momentarily) stop them from considering inappropriate behaviour.

Abstract concepts – concrete activities

One of the greatest skills of the practitioner or teacher is to put across tricky, abstract ideas in such a way that the learners can understand them. We take an abstract concept (numbers, forces, metaphors, population spread) and find a real-life, concrete, meaningful way to make this idea come to life.

A key cause of inappropriate behaviour is when the learners can't access the learning. They get frustrated or embarrassed at not understanding, and they mess around to hide this. By creating concrete activities, where the learners *do* and then *understand*, you make the learning far more accessible for your class.

The younger your learners, the more concrete you need to make the activities you use. With very young children you take the concepts right back to their most basic form. Let's look at three concepts from different age ranges and subjects, which you might want to put across to your learners.

Foundation Stage

Abstract concept – that writing (letters and numbers) can be used to convey meaning.

Practical activity: the practitioner sets up a 'shop' area in the role-play corner, and adds sticky notes, clipboards and pens. They talk with the children about how they might write 'price tickets' to go on the different items.

Primary science

Abstract concept – push, pull and forces (Newton's Third Law).

Practical activity: the teacher offers the learners a range of different wheeled resources – a skateboard, a toy car, a buggy, and some other items, such as a fan, a magnet and a rope. The learners are challenged to find as many different ways to move the wheeled objects as they can.

Secondary history

Abstract concept – eyewitness accounts are often unreliable.

Practical activity: The teacher liaises with a helper ahead of time. The lesson begins by a discussion with the learners about why eyewitness accounts might be unreliable. Suddenly, the helper bursts into the room, runs up to the teacher, gives them a pretend smack across the face and then runs out again. The teacher asks the class to write an eyewitness account – what did they just see, what did the person look like, what were they wearing, and so on? The class compares accounts and then the helper comes back in so that they can judge their accuracy.

Where possible, add other elements to your concrete activities – make them multisensory, colourful, eye-catching, topical. The more of these techniques you get in place, the more likely your learners are to fully engage with learning.

The delivery of lessons

Effective lesson delivery is as much about teacher style and personality as it is about good planning. Aim to communicate:

- a sense of passion for the subject, the topic or the skill being learnt
- a love of the process of learning
- a sense of curiosity about, and interest in, the world
- the feeling that you are really interested in the learners and you want them to be successful
- the feeling that your job as an educator *really matters* to you.

The amount of energy and enthusiasm you put into your work has a direct impact on how your learners feel about being with you. Some days it's hard to find the energy but it's worth it when you can.

The importance of time management

The way you control time can have a surprisingly powerful effect on behaviour, either positive or negative. Follow the dos and don'ts below to get this area of your practice just right.

Do:

✔ Take a calm, measured approach.

✔ Give each activity a suitable amount of time – not too long or too short.

✔ Be flexible about how much you can achieve: adapt to the reality of the situation.

✔ Remember, you'll have to spend some time giving rewards and possibly consequences too.

✔ Take care over the start of lessons or sessions – use a whole-group focus to pull the class together, especially after a break.

✔ Remember, some classes respond well to a 'quick start'; others need to be eased in, perhaps by taking a register.

✔ Consider the end of lessons too. Spend some time on a review, or on calming down your learners if it's been an exciting session.

✔ Aim to finish early – it's far better to eke out the last bit of a lesson than to have to rush after the session time is over.

Don't:

✘ Allow your sessions to feel rushed – you'll stress your learners and they'll be more likely to behave inappropriately.

✘ Plan to do too much during a lesson – you'll end up rushing to fit everything in.

✘ Be in a rush to get started or finished.

✘ Finish late, and have to rush everyone out or clear away yourself.

✘ Send the learners away with their last impression being that of a stressed-out teacher.

A very useful activity for finishing off a session in the right frame of mind is 'statues'. I've used this activity with all ages: from early years right through to adults. Ask the learners to get themselves comfy, and then say 'freeze'. They must now stay completely still for a couple of minutes (or however long is appropriate). On your signal, the learners 'unfreeze' and get ready to go. In primary or secondary school, get them to push their chairs behind the desks, as quietly as possible. Do this in slow motion if you like, to add an element of fun.

Guaranteed to succeed

Sometimes you will just not be up to coping with a really difficult class. On these occasions you need activities and lessons that are pretty much guaranteed to encourage appropriate behaviour. Don't feel guilty about needing the occasional lesson off from coping with poor behaviour. You're only human, and no one can work at full steam all the time. Teaching is, in many ways, like acting: you're presenting yourself to a large (and often difficult) audience. Nobody would realistically expect an actor to perform all day every day – the same applies to the exhausted teacher.

The suggestions below are practically guaranteed to succeed, even with the most difficult learners/classes. They have worked for me in a variety of schools, from the 'fairly easy' to the 'downright impossible'.

- **The computer:** put a learner of any age in front of a laptop and you'll get, at the very least, a bit of peace and quiet. There's loads of great learning that can take place too – research via the internet, creating PowerPoint slides, making a leaflet.

- **Film clips and documentaries:** a primary-school teacher once told me in an interview that to get through in the toughest schools 'we watched more TV than was strictly necessary'. Even the 'class from hell' will usually sit fairly quietly to watch a video. Assuage your guilt by ensuring it's related to a subject they are studying. Make sure it's up to date, interesting enough to keep their attention and test out the technology ahead of time.

- **Outside visitors:** learners often respond really well to people who are not in the role of 'teacher'. It takes a bit of forward-planning, but when you have a visitor it gives you a bit of a break. It's often really inspirational for your learners as well. It could be a theatre group, a police officer, a parent with an exciting career, a yoga specialist, or a conservation group that brings in birds of prey for the learners to handle.

As well as bringing in visitors from outside, make sure you ask around for volunteers who might be willing to support you in your setting. Many early years settings and primary schools have lots of parent/carer volunteers helping out. The more adults in the room, the more eyes there are to watch out for any signs of inappropriate behaviour!

Engaging activities across the curriculum

This section gives you a few ideas that I have used, or seen used, to engage a difficult (and, indeed, an easy) class. When I say 'engage', what I mean is to make the learners so interested in and focused on the learning, that they seem to forget about behaving inappropriately. To get your learners engaged, what you're after is something that falls into one of the following categories:

- bizarre
- weird
- surprising
- unusual
- strange but true
- fascinating
- gripping
- thrilling
- yucky
- crazy
- true to life.

You're also looking for something with all those elements I discussed earlier on in this chapter – multisensory, topical, and so on.

The scene of the crime

Areas of learning

- creative and lateral thinking
- examining evidence
- close observation
- analysis, deduction and theorising
- studying texts
- the crime genre
- mapping and drawing plans
- forensics, samples, fair testing
- discussion and decision-making

Resources

- an open area (push any chairs or desks aside)
- police 'crime scene' tape (you can buy this from online shops or from www.uktapes.com)
- props relating to the crime (a handbag with the contents spilt out, a bottle, a length of rope, money – whatever you like really)
- plastic gloves (I save them when I fill up my car with petrol)
- 'police report' form

Description

I originally devised this activity to teach the crime genre in drama: it grabs the attention of even the most difficult class. Your learners should quite readily go along with the 'fiction' of the lesson. When they enter the room, tell them that there has been a crime. They must not touch anything (though they will want to) – ask them why and they'll tell you all about fingerprints.

With older learners, your crime could be a more serious one; with young ones, choose a gentler idea – the class toy has been taken, a pot of pencils has gone missing, someone has eaten the porridge!

The learners work as police detectives to examine the crime scene. They discuss their findings, backing up their suppositions with an analysis of the evidence (that makes it sound tricky but it can be done with learners of any age, working at different levels of complexity). You can develop this activity in lots of ways, depending on the curriculum area you want to work on:

- Draw a detailed plan of the crime scene.
- Measure footprints to work out the height of the criminal.
- Complete a 'police report', listing evidence, identifying witnesses.
- Interview a suspect, recording the discussion.
- Film a dramatic TV reconstruction of the crime.
- Test forensic samples.
- Stage a court case, with judge, lawyers, defendant, etc.

As well as being a useful generic activity, you can also link this into specific texts. In English, I've used it to study Shakespeare's *Romeo and Juliet* by setting up the 'crime scene' from the end of the story. I've also used it to explore some of the Sherlock Holmes detective stories.

The can of dog food

Areas of learning

- marketing and the power of persuasion (should we always believe what we read on the label?)
- design and art skills
- what's on a label
- tamper-proof packaging
- analysis of samples

Resources

- a can of dog food or a pouch of cat food
- chopped-up Mars bars
- orange jelly
- a fork
- tape or glue

Description

This activity was originally used for design technology, and it shocks the learners into paying attention. Of all the suggestions I've ever made, this has attracted the most controversy. Your teaching style probably needs to be 'comic and quirky' or possibly 'on the edge' to pull it off. Prepare your can ahead of time: cut the base off the tin or split open the pouch carefully; empty it out and wash it well; chop up the Mars bars and mix this with the jelly; refill the can or pouch and fix it back together with glue or tape. (Note: an easier alternative is to swap the labels over between dog food and something more appetising.)

Explain to the class that the lesson is about packaging. Show the learners the can of dog food, open it up, and then eat from it. Offer it round the class, to see if anyone will have a taste. You'll get a lively reaction to this opening, but your learners will eventually quieten down, because they want to find out what's going on. You could move on to:

- Discuss the 'power of persuasion' and how marketing affects us.
- Explore what's on different labels and what it tells us.
- Test the contents of various cans to see what they contain.
- Design your own labels.

The market

Areas of learning

- speaking and listening, building vocabulary
- using the target language in modern foreign languages
- money, prices, adding, subtracting
- art, design, creative skills

- drama, characterisation and improvisation
- understanding of other cultures (foods, clothes)

Resources

- tables to use as market stalls
- food or other goods for the stalls
- money (real or toy)
- tills if you have them
- paper and pens to create signs

Description

This lesson was originally set in a French market place to get the learners practising their language skills. The learners set up stalls selling foods or goods. They act as stall-holders or visitors to the market, buying and selling goods. You can adapt this activity to use in a range of subject areas or with different age groups. Your learners could:

- Act out some scenes from the market in a drama session.
- Design and create signs to show what the different stalls sell.
- Use your market for a role play based in different parts of the world, selling the appropriate foods or goods.
- Learn and practise specific vocabulary or phrases in a target language, related to buying and selling.
- Use this as a numeracy or maths activity, using money, calculating profit.
- Set up the stalls as a small business venture with a business studies class.

Bring this activity to life by getting your learners to set up some real stalls in your setting, for instance, selling drinks at break times.

Using resources

Resources bring the learning to life: learners love them, especially anything that's out of the ordinary. When you bring in an inspirational resource this can impact on behaviour, because it engages your learners and encourages them to focus on the activity. In the Foundation Stage, teachers facilitate learning through the way that they resource the space – the children access what is made available to them. But resources are important for learners of every age. Even adults love to handle something while they learn. As well as choosing the right resources, to get the right results you need to think about using them in an imaginative way.

Resources come in all different shapes and sizes:

- natural or 'found' objects, such as pebbles, shells or leaves
- man-made objects, such as toys and educational resources
- equipment – rulers, blocks, balance beams
- paper, cardboard, collage materials
- paints, pens, other mark-making equipment
- props, and other 'dramatic' items
- costumes, wigs, hats, make-up
- people – support staff, visitors, experts, other learners
- displays
- sound and lighting – soundtracks, torches
- cameras, tablets and other technological equipment.

Treat your resources in a creative way. A cardboard box could be:

- turned into a spaceship – decorate it, play inside it, do the count-down for 'blast off!'
- presented as a 'magic box' – the learners must cast the right spell to open it
- designed to be the box for a fantastic new cereal
- taken apart to look at how it's constructed
- filled up with smaller items, to learn about volume and estimating.

As well as giving resources to your learners, you can also use them yourself. Dress up as a famous figure from history or as a character from a book. Use resources to inspire your learners and make them forget all about behaving inappropriately.

Part Three

The Learners and the Setting

Chapter 8
The Learners

Dealing with different types of learners

This chapter looks in detail at the learners you work with, whether they are young children, primary-aged pupils, secondary learners, teenagers, young people or adult learners. I look at why learners might struggle to behave, the strategies you can use to stop this happening, and approaches to deal with inappropriate behaviour when it does occur. You'll find case studies, designed to bring each issue to life and to show you how the ideas could work in a real-life situation.

Every learner you teach is an interesting and complex individual. It is possible to make some general observations though, to help you deal with difficult behaviour. The policy of inclusion means that you will come across learners with a wide range of needs in mainstream classrooms. Some will have fairly high-level behavioural difficulties that in the past might have been handled in a specialist setting. The more you understand about the different needs that your learners have, the more confident you will feel about supporting them.

Why do learners behave inappropriately?

When a learner behaves inappropriately, there may be several contributing factors. Considering what these might be does not mean that you are excusing the behaviour, or blaming yourself for it; considering these underlying factors can give you insights into what you might be able to do to solve the issues. Below is a list of potential causes:

Factors from outside the setting

- Parents or carers had a negative experience of school themselves, and have passed on this negativity to their children.
- There is little or no support for learning and school in the home.

- Parents or carers struggled to set clear boundaries around behaviour in the child's early years, for instance, because of their home context or poor mental health.
- The young person has suffered adverse childhood experiences which had an impact developmentally, for instance, for a looked-after child who has been removed from their birth parents.
- There are bleak prospects on offer beyond education in the local area, so it feels pointless to young people to try.

Factors from inside the setting

- The ethos of the setting is ill-defined – leaders are not in control and learners have the sense that they can do what they want.
- The behaviour policy is not working effectively and needs adapting to the context. The behaviour policy is not being consistently applied, for instance, because of lack of staff training or 'buy-in'.
- The sheer weight of numbers of learners with serious behaviour issues makes it hard for the school to get a handle on the problem.

Factors relating to the teacher

- A tendency to 'wind up' the learners and get them overexcited.
- Uncertainty about the behaviour the teacher wants to see.
- Overreacting to minor inappropriate behaviour, tending towards a confrontational approach.
- High levels of stress caused by problem behaviour leading to a negative feeling.
- Lessons are pitched at the wrong level, so learners can't access them.

Factors relating to the learner

- They have learning difficulties, and find it hard to access the work. These may not have been diagnosed.
- They have social, emotional or mental health challenges and find it extra difficult to behave appropriately.
- They lack motivation to learn, or have never learnt the skills of self-discipline and focus.
- They perceive learning as boring or meaningless.

- Negative peer pressure has a powerful influence within the group.
- There is low self-esteem, either individually or within the group.
- The learners want to wind the teacher up – and they know that they can.

Learner case studies

To show you how you might deal effectively with individual learners, here are some case studies. I've alternated the gender here, so that these use a balance of male and female learners. In each case study:

- I give an example of a particular type of behaviour.
- I explore some of the reasons this inappropriate behaviour might occur, including the SEND which the behaviour could flag up for you.
- I discuss the kind of problems you might experience with this learner.
- I suggest strategies to try when working with the learner, and generally when working with learners who have this type of difficulty.
- I use examples from a variety of age groups.

Case study: the distracted learner who lacks focus

The learner (early years)

Jenna is a sweet child, but finds it very hard to stay focused. When you play alongside her she can concentrate for a little while, but as soon as you move away she gets distracted. You sometimes find her staring out of the window, lost to the world. Jenna struggles to sit still for carpet/circle time. Unless an adult sits with her, she often just wanders away. She doesn't speak very much and her language development is delayed.

What causes distraction/lack of focus?

- Never being encouraged at home to focus on one single activity for an extended period.
- Too many toys in the home, or too few.
- Not much experience of playing together with others (carers, friends).
- Physical factors – tiredness, not eating enough, or eating the wrong things.
- Too much screen time – lots of TV or computer games.
- Behavioural needs arising out of SEND, for instance, processing difficulties.

Specific strategies for helping Jenna

- Encourage Jenna to develop her focus. When you talk with her, hold eye contact and use plenty of tone to engage her.

- Pay her individual attention, greeting her by name when she arrives at your setting. Have a task and a target for arrival time. For instance, her parents or carers could help her self-register, and praise her when she manages to do this.

- At carpet time, get a member of staff to sit with her to help her focus. Alternatively, give her a little job to do, such as setting out the cups for drinks.

- Work out where Jenna's strengths and interests lie, and set up some play-based activities in your provision around these areas to boost her focus.

- Do some short 'focus' activities with the group, for instance, playing statues or practising physical skills such as using a balancing beam.

- Incorporate visual methods into the approaches you use with Jenna – pictures to show your setting routine, toy boxes labelled with photos.

- Speak to Jenna's parents or carers to explain how they can support Jenna at home.

- Get your special educational needs coordinator (SENCO) to observe Jenna's behaviour to see whether she might have additional needs that are causing the lack of focus.

General techniques for helping distracted learners

- Examine your planning to make sure children don't have to listen or focus on one task for an overly long time.

- Give the learner something to fiddle with (a pipe cleaner, some Plasticine) when you talk to the whole group.

- Offer volunteer tasks that keep the learner active and involved.

- Use plenty of hands-on approaches in lessons.

- Divide the work up into short activities. Set time limits for each one, with rewards for completion of each task.

- Ensure that the learner understands the activities you set – make time for a short one-to-one so they are sure of what to do.

- Find a responsible partner or friend with whom the learner enjoys working, and ask them to help her stay on task.

- Use an egg timer to give the learner a visual aid when doing a task. Ask them to raise a hand once the sand has run through, to prompt you to go and check in with them.

- Build up the length of time of tasks, as a learner gradually develops their focus.

- Use visual indicators to help the learner understand the passing of time. For instance, an individual timetable with coloured symbols, stuck to a desk.

- Speak to SEND colleagues and get their advice. Could the inability to focus be a symptom of an unidentified special educational need?

If your learner has been identified as having Attention Deficit Disorder (ADD) or Attention Deficit Hyperactivity Disorder (ADHD), read up about this type of difficulty. Learners with ADHD may take medication, usually a stimulant, to help control the symptoms. If the symptoms are severe, the learner might have a statement of special educational needs.

Many of the strategies in this book will automatically be beneficial for learners with ADHD or autism. Techniques such as using clear routines, applying boundaries consistently and setting well-structured tasks are all part of helping these learners cope.

Case study: the learner who doesn't understand

The learner (lower primary)

When Sundip arrived at school he spoke very little to staff or other children. He has just moved into your Year 2 class. He is speaking a bit now, but his writing is very weak and he can only just write his name. He struggles with reading and gets very frustrated when he can't work out what a word says. He disrupts whole-class carpet time by annoying the child sitting next to him on the carpet, or getting up and wandering around the room. When asked a question by the teacher, Sundip looks blank and refuses to answer.

What causes lack of understanding?

- Various special educational needs can lead to a lack of understanding, particularly needs related to communication, language and literacy, such as developmental language disorder (DLD).

- It could be that a young learner does not understand your vocabulary; perhaps an older learner cannot read what you write on the board.

- Perhaps the learner hasn't had the necessary stimulation at home – if no one talks to them or reads with them, the school needs to put in a lot of time developing language skills.

- Learners with English as an additional language (EAL) might speak little at first and find it harder to understand the teacher.

- It could be that the learner has a physical disability which has not been diagnosed – for instance, they can't see the board or find it hard to hear what you're saying.

Some learners are adept at covering up difficulties with literacy. They behave inappropriately to avoid having to show their lack of understanding and get a reputation for being 'difficult'. This becomes a vicious cycle. The learner behaves inappropriately because they don't understand; because they're behaving, they don't access the learning. The longer this goes on, the more entrenched the situation becomes.

Specific strategies for helping Sundip

- Speak as a matter of urgency to your SENCO and Sundip's previous class teacher. Find out exactly what his learning needs are.
- Read his special needs documentation (if there is some). If there isn't, note down and flag up your concerns with your SENCO.
- Create differentiated tasks, or use scaffolds, so that the learning is at a level Sundip can access.
- Where possible, give Sundip one-to-one support to help him get onto task and focus on his learning. Ignore low-level attention-seeking behaviour from Sundip.
- Ask yourself, 'Is this immediately interfering with my ability to teach the class?' If not, try deferring your response to the problem and focusing on praising other learners instead.
- Use clear, simple language with Sundip and speak slowly. Back up what you say with gestures.
- Set straightforward targets for Sundip, and create an individualised reward system for him. Reward every step to boost his confidence.
- Consider an intervention to get Sundip's reading up to speed.
- Use plenty of discussion activities: the more Sundip's speaking develops, the more confident he will be about his writing.

General techniques for helping learners who don't understand

- Use differentiated activities and adaptive teaching to give every learner a chance to succeed in your lessons.
- Use technology to help learners – if a learner finds handwriting or spelling very challenging, writing at times on a laptop can be helpful to improve motivation.

- Flag up concerns as soon as you have them. Don't hold back on doing this – many learners go through school with an unidentified difficulty. Once it's identified, they can get the help they need.

- Be conscious of the learner's emotions: never embarrass them or draw attention to a particular weakness in front of the class.

- Make allowances, but don't excuse all inappropriate behaviour as being caused by lack of understanding. You won't do your learners any favours if you don't set clear targets and boundaries for them. Just be flexible in your approach to achieving those targets.

- With adult learners, be aware that they might have a very negative experience of education, particularly if they struggled at school and didn't get the help they needed.

- Find a chance for the learner to shine – everyone is good at *something*. Find out what that something is and let your learners express their talents.

- Keep yourself up to date with best practice in different areas of SEND, by going on training courses whenever you can.

Case study: the learner who lacks motivation and interest

The learner (upper primary)

Katriona just can't seem to be bothered. She rarely completes any work, despite you applying consequences from the school behaviour system. If she does finish something, it is scrappy and of poor quality. She regularly 'forgets' to bring her kit for PE. When questioned as to why she hasn't completed a task, Katriona will say, 'I couldn't be bothered' or 'it was boring'.

You've tried using rewards to encourage Katriona, but she doesn't respond to the rewards that work with other learners in the class. The only time you've ever seen Katriona really enthusiastic was when a nature group visited school with some exotic insects. Her picture of the praying mantis won a prize in an art competition.

What causes lack of motivation and interest?

- Some learners just aren't that interested in school, perhaps as a result of their parents or carers not seeing any value in education.

- As they approach secondary-school age, some learners move into the hormonal rollercoaster of puberty, and this has an effect on their energy and motivation levels.

- If a learner isn't eating or sleeping properly, this can cause an apathetic approach. For instance, if their parents or carers aren't aware that they are staying up late gaming.

- Some learners will disguise their lack of understanding by saying that they 'can't be bothered', when what they really mean is they 'can't do it'.

- If the teacher lacks energy or has got into bad habits, this can mean that individual learners or a whole class become switched off in the lessons.

- Sometimes school is actually just a bit boring; unfortunately, learners need to learn to cope with this reality.

Specific strategies for helping Katriona

- Check with your SENCO to find out whether Katriona has any learning needs: perhaps she is covering up a difficulty.

- Make sure it's not something simple – have a chat with Katriona and her parents about whether she is eating and sleeping properly. They might actually welcome some advice and support on bedtime routines.

- Set Katriona short, achievable targets during lessons. Draw a line on the page and ask her to write down to it.

- Give her an instant reward, such as verbal praise or a sticker, each time she meets a target.

- Talk to Katriona about which rewards would motivate her – adapt the school system to suit her needs.

- Try to give Katriona some one-to-one support. Talk her through exactly what she needs to do and reinforce how well she is doing.

- If appropriate, sit Katriona with a well-motivated partner or friend who can help and encourage her.

- Find out what really interests Katriona and incorporate some of this into your lesson-planning.

- Find ways for Katriona to gain a feeling of success. Ask her what she enjoyed about the insect visit and think about how you could replicate this.

- Art is clearly an interest for her – capitalise on this to motivate Katriona, for instance, by asking her to help you create a display.

- Consider letting Katriona use a laptop to write on for some activities. Try this as a motivator for completing a specific amount of written work.

General techniques for helping learners who lack motivation

- Make the learning the driver to get your learners motivated.
- Use creative, imaginative and inspirational approaches.
- Maintain a relentlessly positive approach yourself, modelling the ambition and high standards you want your learners to achieve.
- Put as much enthusiasm as possible into the way that you deal with the class.
- If it's a whole class that seems unmotivated, it is hard to stay positive. But it's far better than the alternative: giving up and letting negativity win.
- Think about the pace of your lessons. Move quickly into the session, using your voice and body to give energy and forward momentum.
- When you organise an activity, be clear about the target for how much work should be done, and how long the learners have to complete it.
- Choose short time limits and targets over longer ones, to inject a feeling of pace.
- Think about the overall look of your room – a bright and fresh space can push us into having more get-up-and-go.
- If your overall setting is dull, drab or dilapidated, make your own teaching space an oasis of colour and delight.
- Do something original and daring and completely new with the class. Think laterally and come up with something out of the ordinary, to show your learners that education is worth it.

Case study: the aggressive and confrontational learner

The learner (lower secondary)

Ryan is known throughout school. Other teachers frequently refer to his aggressive and antisocial behaviour in their classes. He is a large, powerfully built boy, and you sometimes feel physically threatened by him. At the slightest provocation, Ryan starts to shout and cause problems. He acts negatively towards the other members of the class, and they have told you that they are becoming scared of him. You've been warned not to contact the home because his parents also have a reputation for aggression.

Ryan rarely does any work in your lessons, but when you try to discipline him, he reacts in a hostile manner. You've tried giving him rewards, with some success, but Ryan very quickly drops back into a confrontational attitude.

What causes aggression and confrontation?

- Most learners who are aggressive or confrontational have developed these behaviours from seeing them modelled at home.

- If the adults in their lives always react aggressively behaviour, the child quickly picks this up and copies them.

- Some learners let off steam in school or college, because they would be too afraid to do this at home. The teacher becomes a safety valve for what are effectively safeguarding or child protection issues.

- Some learners find it hard to manage their anger, and have never learnt strategies for self-calming.

- Some learners have poor impulse control, and a tendency to react in an emotional way.

Specific strategies for helping Ryan

- Check whether Ryan has been assessed as having special educational needs. Find out from SEN staff what sets him off.

- Arrange some anger management classes for Ryan. Let the leadership team know that staff and learners feel threatened by his behaviour.

- Talk to Ryan (or the whole class) about different ways to manage anger and emotional reactions, practising these together. Simple things like counting to ten or breathing deeply are a great help.

- Don't confront Ryan: it's not worth the risk to your own safety.

- Aim to remain calm and use low-key approaches. Ignore minor poor behaviours as appropriate.

- Create a 'get-out' option for Ryan: if he feels he is going to blow, arrange for him to go and sit with a senior member of staff.

- Perhaps staff tend to react to Ryan's size and physical presence, and expect him to cause trouble. Give yourself permission to avoid focusing on Ryan and the problems he creates for you.

- Document all incidents involving Ryan, especially if he threatens you or uses aggressive or violent behaviour. Pass on copies of this information to the leadership team and special needs staff.

- If you feel things are getting out of hand, and you are in danger of being assaulted, discuss this with a senior leader or union representative.

General techniques for helping aggressive/confrontational learners

- Offer a calm, consistent and positive role model from which the learner can see a different model.

- Greet the learner by name at the start of lessons; mention your positive expectations of what they will achieve.

- Be as consistent as possible about your expectations, but apply flexibility when it proves necessary. Don't put yourself in danger.

- Avoid shouting – this exacerbates confrontational behaviour.

- Catch the learner behaving well and praise them for it. Don't wait for a negative incident to focus on them.

- Set achievable targets for work or behaviour and reward the learner for completion of each one.

- Consider seating arrangements – it might be best to seat this learner as close to your desk as possible.

- With a particularly aggressive individual, have a back-up plan whereby you remove yourself and others from danger.

You can find the most up-to-date government guidance on the use of reasonable force online. Read this information, putting yourself in a position where you know what you can and cannot do. Then, when an incident occurs and a learner says to you, 'you can't touch me' you'll be able to explain exactly why their behaviour might mean that, in law, you can.

Case study: the learner with social issues

The learner (upper secondary)

Madison is an unusual learner, newly arrived at the school. You see her wandering around the school alone at break- and lunchtimes – she has not bonded with her peer group at all. Her uniform is tatty and dirty, and you've heard learners saying she needs to use deodorant.

Although Madison's individual work is of a good quality, she finds it hard to learn in a group. None of the other learners wants to work with her, and a few of them have approached you to request that you stop putting her in their group.

When you talk to Madison individually, she finds it hard to make eye contact, and she mumbles her answers. Madison is not doing anything 'wrong' as such; her behaviour is worrying rather than disruptive. Her strange behaviour is starting to have an impact on the atmosphere in the class.

What causes social issues?

- Some learners find it hard to socialise and get on with their peers. This may be because they have not had experience of doing this in early childhood.

- If a learner is on the autism spectrum, this can cause difficulties with learning social skills and understanding social situations.

- Social issues can also be related to neglect and child protection concerns.

- At times of transition, learners have to fit into new social groupings, and this can lead to issues with making friends.

- In some schools, there is a culture of negativity towards learners who work hard and behave well.

- Bullying can also be a factor in these circumstances.

Specific strategies for helping Madison

- From the evidence in the case study, it sounds as though Madison might be experiencing neglect. Speak to the school's designated safeguarding lead (DSL) to flag up your concerns.

- For a while, hold back a bit from activities that require group work. Aim to get Madison settled into the class as a priority.

- Aim to find out whether there is any bullying going on. Follow the school's procedures for identifying and dealing with this.

- When you use group work, have an expectation that everyone works with everyone, despite any personal preferences. Don't give in to learners who complain.

- Make it clear that you are not willing to put up with bullying, and that everyone in the class must be given equal respect.

- Build up Madison's confidence, praising her by using written comments when she does a good piece of work. Try not to let other learners witness the praise: they may see this as further reason to isolate her.

- Spend time talking to Madison individually during lessons, gradually winning her trust and getting her to learn how to make eye contact. Coax her gently as she is clearly fragile.

- See if you can identify one or two kinder members of the class who might be able to befriend Madison.

- Some schools use more general techniques to support socialisation, for instance, having a 'friendship bench' in the playground to encourage kinder attitudes to peers.

General techniques for helping learners with social issues

- Talk to the class generally about how important it is to accept and respect anybody and everybody. Don't mention any individuals by name; just discuss how it would feel to be left out of a group.

- Do whole-class personal, social and health education (PSHE) activities around bullying and friendship issues. Make it completely clear that you will not accept any incidents of bullying in your class. Talk about the consequences for those who do bully.

- If you have a group of learners who don't fit into the peer group, they might appreciate it if you offer a volunteer task which allows them to stay in at break. This could be tidying a cupboard or organising some displays. For learners who are ostracised from the bulk of the peer group, break times can be lonely and frightening.

- Look for ways to boost the confidence of learners with social issues or low self-esteem. Encourage them to get involved in extracurricular activities, finding something that they enjoy. This could be a debating society, a poetry club, a school show, The Duke of Edinburgh Award, helping run a club for younger learners, and so on.

Case study: the learner who is deliberately disruptive

The learner (further education)

Josh is almost impossible to teach. When he does turn up (always late) he immediately disrupts your lesson. He winds up the other learners or gets them to join him in messing around. He acts aggressively towards the quieter members of the class. He rarely does any work, and when he does complete a task, you often find it contains rude, personal comments about you.

When you try to discipline Josh, he responds negatively, swearing at you and insulting you. You've been in several arguments with him, and he always wants the final say. He's already told you that college is a waste of time. You're reaching breaking point, and dread facing Josh in your lessons.

What causes deliberately disruptive behaviour?

- Often, a number of factors come together to create disruptive behaviour, particularly where it is deliberate.

- Typically, the learner has not been successful early on in school, perhaps because of learning needs that were not identified.

- It's likely that the learner comes from a home background where boundaries are inconsistent or non-existent.

- As the learner progresses through school, failing and getting in trouble, it's understandable that they feel like a 'marked person'.

- They learn to live up to their reputation and get some measure of satisfaction from winding up the teacher.

- The learner typically values their status within the peer group, and relishes being able to control or even turn the group against the teacher.

- Sometimes the teacher perceives the inappropriate behaviour as deliberate when actually it is part of a larger SEND issue.

Specific strategies for helping Josh

- Document everything – write an account of the day, time, what Josh said and did, send copies to the relevant people. Include the inclusion support team, your line manager, your faculty leader, and so on.

- Check with SEND staff to see whether there is something specific about Josh's background or learning needs that you should know.

- Follow your college disciplinary procedures to the letter, even if that means that Josh gets removed from your lessons. Don't feel guilty about this: why should you and the other learners have to put up with aggressive behaviour?

- Ask other staff how they deal with Josh. Find out what, if anything, is currently being done to help him change his behaviour.

- The rest of the class is probably fed up with Josh as well. Before he arrives, talk to the rest of your learners about what they could do to help him improve. Suggest that they ignore his behaviour and focus on their own learning instead.

- Catch Josh being good (if it ever happens). Public praise might be useful here, especially if he responds well to peer-group approval.

- Don't get into arguments with Josh. Be the one to walk away, rather than trying to reason with him when he won't listen.

- Don't hesitate to bring in a senior member of staff to help you deal with the situation if necessary. If it comes to the stage where you feel threatened, call for help immediately.

General techniques for helping deliberately disruptive learners

- Accept that there are some learners who decide to wind up the teacher and disrupt lessons. Feel pity for them, but don't waste your energy getting angry. You can't change the world for every single learner.

- Follow your school or college procedures to the letter, staying calm and rational throughout (there's *no* point in allowing yourself to get wound up).

- Blame the policy, not the learner – keep it depersonalised.

- Focus on what you are there for – to teach.

- Contact parents or carers if they are likely to be supportive. But be careful – often the learner's behaviour is a result of his upbringing and contacting the home could make things worse.

- Don't take this type of behaviour personally, or allow it to make you become defensive. Typically, it is not personal, but a reaction against an education system that the learner feels has failed them.

- Do what you can to help, but don't let this learner drain all your energy. Focus on the hard-working, positive learners instead.

Learners and special educational needs staff

There are many different special needs staff working in the education system, all of whom should be happy to help you support your learners and meet their needs. Depending on the size and type of your organisation, you may have:

- a SENCo (sometimes titled SENDCo)
- special needs assistants
- learning support staff
- educational welfare officers
- learning support officers
- counsellors.

Your setting will also be working in conjunction with other agencies and professionals, including:

- educational psychologists
- speech and language therapists

- social workers
- child protection professionals.

Get to know these people: ask for help or for more detailed information on individual learners. Sometimes confidentiality means they can't be too specific, but they can give you general advice on what works best.

As a teacher/practitioner, you are vital because you work day to day with the learners. It is your role to flag up any learners whose needs have not yet been identified. Learners can develop difficulties at any time in their education: keep an eye out for any learners who are experiencing problems with learning which might impact on their behaviour.

Some teachers have a member of the SEN staff working in the classroom, for instance, a learning support assistant (LSA) who is working one-to-one with a child who has an EHCP (Education Health and Care Plan). Many primary teachers now have at least a part-time teaching assistant to support them. If this is the case for you:

- Plan ahead together, wherever possible, to make the best use of support-staff time.
- Share your lesson plans in advance.
- Ask for help in adapting activities to suit individuals with particular needs.
- Ask support staff how they want to work – perhaps withdrawing a few learners from the class, working with groups, or with specific individuals.
- In theory, the person with the highest level of qualifications in the class should work with those learners who have the highest levels of needs. Avoid always putting your LSA with the lowest attaining learners and groups, since you are probably more highly qualified as a teacher.

Learners and transitions

There are various transition points for learners during their education. For instance, they might move:

- from home to a preschool or nursery
- from nursery or preschool to a primary school
- from the Foundation Stage to Key Stage 1 (in England)
- from infant to middle or junior school
- from primary to secondary school
- from secondary school to sixth form or college.

Around each of these points, learners can experience issues with behaviour, whether it's to do with handling the change, or with moving from one situation to another, very different one. Their learning can also suffer, either standing still or even dropping back. At transition points, learners have to:

- find their way around a new place
- get to know new people (both staff and peers)
- get to know the layout of the buildings
- understand how the new setting runs
- learn new systems and routines.

Generally speaking, learners who are new to a setting are more malleable, and can be moulded to your way of thinking, behaving and working. By the time they reach the last year of any setting, however, learners are at the top of the school. Their increased status means they often begin to test the boundaries.

Research suggests that one of the most important factors in mitigating difficulties around transitions is communication. Where you are working with a group who are about to transition to a new setting, talk with learners about what to expect and what the new systems will be like. Ask them about their worries or concerns and arrange transition visits with the new setting, as well as ensuring that information about SEND gets shared.

Chapter 9
The Teaching Space

The environment and behaviour

Think for a moment about how the space you live in affects the way you feel. If your home is busy, cramped or noisy, you get stressed more easily. People get under each other's feet and feelings run high. If you live in a cluttered, untidy and dirty environment, you can feel depressed and mentally overcrowded as well. If, on the other hand, you live in an open, spacious, light and airy space, with a wonderful view, this inevitably puts you in a positive, relaxed and happy mood.

We saw this effect magnified during the early pandemic lockdowns – those learners who were from the most disadvantaged backgrounds had the hardest time learning from home. There was often a lack of suitable spaces in which to learn, or a lack of suitable technology and other resources, and this clearly impacted directly on their progress.

From the moment they arrive at your room, your learners are making conscious and subconscious judgements about what to expect from you, by what they first see of you and your space. You want to create the feeling of a calm, positive, ordered environment, where the teacher is in control. While there is much about our teaching spaces that we cannot change, there are many ways we can improve how our rooms look and consequently the behaviour of our learners within them.

Your learners' behaviour is affected by:

- the way your teaching environment appears
- the way you set out and structure the space
- how the resources and equipment within the space are organised
- how you move around the space.

In this chapter, I look at ways in which the physical environment of the classroom can be used and improved to have a positive impact on behaviour. As well as helping you to handle learner behaviour, your teaching space should hopefully help you to stay calm, happy and relaxed.

Please note: I use the term 'space' in this chapter to describe the whole range of different teaching spaces – from classrooms to halls, drama studios to gymnasiums, lecture theatres to labs, nurseries to schools.

Improving the environment

Your learners should perceive your space as a safe, calm place where learning can and will take place. If they do, they will be more likely to focus on learning and less likely to behave inappropriately. If you teach in the early years or in the primary sector, this is the place where your children will spend the majority of each session or day. Similarly, if you teach older learners, this is the place where you will spend a lot of your time (unless you are one of the unfortunate teachers without a teaching space of your own). Each class that visits you in your room should find you in control of a wonderful 'haven of learning'.

Some settings are modern, well-designed, open, airy spaces, full of light and well maintained. Others are dingy, old-fashioned and run down. However, there are always plenty of things that you can do to improve any environment. Whatever your teaching space is like, you owe it to yourself and your learners to improve the environment as much as you can.

To get the best behaviour, work to make your space:

- welcoming
- tidy and uncluttered
- well organised
- well resourced
- clearly defined
- comfortable and safe
- fun, colourful, engaging, multisensory
- personal to you.

Let's look at each of those points in turn.

Welcoming

First impressions count. Make a good visual impression using signs and displays. 'Welcome' your learners and their parents or carers in different community languages. If you have your own room, put a sign on the door with your name, class and/or class name. View your room as though you are seeing it for the first time – what would you notice first? Are any areas untidy or unwelcoming, or is anything missing?

Tidy and uncluttered

A tidy environment helps you to have a tidy teaching style. You and your learners can find what you need easily, and this creates a calm, controlled feeling. A tidy, uncluttered space gives your learners the perception of order and structure, which in turn helps you to build routines.

Well organised

In an early years or primary space, set up 'stations' for different areas, with resources in clearly labelled drawers ready for learners to access. Include pictures as well as words on your labels. In secondary, have a specific place to store textbooks and exercise books. Train your learners to begin the session by retrieving their learning materials.

Well resourced

Keep your resources tidy too – set aside time to sort through them regularly. In the early years, where there are lots of toys and other resources, aim for quality rather than quantity, wood over plastic. Open-ended resources, which allow for creative thinking and many uses, are preferable to those with only one purpose.

Clearly defined

Clarify the different areas in your room. In an early years setting, activities from different subjects can happen in different parts of the space (mark-making, art, role play, etc. within the continuous provision). Create a clear divide between these different spaces, 'zoning' the areas to help you control the children, particularly if they are working in different areas of learning at one time. The divide could be created by using:

- different colours
- different types of floor covering
- screens or a barrier
- signs and displays
- tables and resources.

Comfortable and safe

Look at your furniture and consider how comfy your learners are when they're learning. Where possible, ask that your setting invests in good-quality seats, cushions and carpets. If you work with young children or with very challenging learners, ensure your environment is completely safe. Have clear rules about bags and other equipment at the start of lessons. Make sure it's safe for you as well. Ensure that effective risk assessments are in place, and speak to the named health and safety representative if you have any concerns.

Fun, colourful, engaging, multisensory

Think imaginatively to achieve this. Music, lights, sound, costumes, plants, displays: experiment and see what happens. Consider whether all your learners' senses are stimulated when they are in your sessions, and if they're not, what you might be able to do about it. Although this can feel like quite a primary-orientated approach, in fact, adding multisensory items (for instance, plants or textured displays) can also help you to create an appealing environment with older learners.

Personal to you

Bring some personal touches into the room – a favourite photo, an important memento, a much-loved ornament. Give your learners a little insight into you the *person*, as well as you the *teacher*.

Some thoughts on displays

When I go into schools and colleges to run training events, it always amazes me how I get an instant 'feel' for the place, simply through what is on the walls. Displays can send a subtle but distinctive message, either that staff and learners care about the setting, or that people here are too hard pressed to be bothered.

No matter how poor the general condition of your classroom, you can always cheer it up with displays. In fact, displays are a good way of covering up dirty walls or peeling paint. I saw a marvellous display once, where the learners had painted a dramatic war poetry display directly on to the class wall, using a black background and large red poppies (check with your leadership team first). Used well, displays are great for developing your learners' learning, or for rewarding hard work. The best displays have some of the following qualities:

- interesting – brightly coloured, three-dimensional
- creative in their use of space – stuck on windows, pegged on a 'washing line' across the ceiling
- interactive – questions to answer, sticky notes to add, lift-up flaps, textures

- a work in progress – the 'working wall', where the learners add ideas as they learn, related to the learning that's currently happening
- tidy and well cared for – demonstrate respect by replacing pins or sticky tack and repairing rips
- changed regularly – not wallpaper.

Think carefully about where you put your displays, because they can act as a distraction, particularly for learners with processing difficulties. For instance, ensure that you don't surround your interactive whiteboard with too much information, which might distract the learners from what you actually want them to focus on.

With changes to teachers' working conditions since I first wrote this book, the task of preparing displays does not come under the tasks that teachers have to do, and typically gets delegated to others. Remember: you don't have to delegate all of this to a teaching assistant; you can also get the learners involved too. They'll be better motivated to take care of displays if they participate in their creation.

The layout of the space

The layout of the room has a strong effect on learners' behaviour and learning, and on their perceptions of what will happen inside the space. For instance, when I ask early years teachers where most of the inappropriate behaviours happen in their settings, they always mention the construction area, and it's interesting to talk to them about why this might be. Depending on your age range and the subject(s) you teach, you might have to decide how to set out desks and chairs, or stools and lab benches, or perhaps a whole range of furniture and equipment in a Foundation Stage or primary classroom. You can, of course, change the layout of the space for different types of activity, getting the learners to help you move things around.

Here are some thoughts about how learners perceive different layouts, and their potential impact on learning and behaviour. In these examples I've assumed a teacher working in a classroom with desks and chairs.

The desks in rows
Advantages

✔ Perceived as 'traditional' by both teachers and learners.

✔ Can be a 'safe option' if you're having trouble controlling behaviour.

✔ It is relatively easy to spot chatter or low-level poor behaviour.

✔ The learners can all see the board.

✔ Resources, books, etc. can be passed along the rows.

✔ It also makes it easier to draw up a seating plan.

Disadvantages

✘ Perceived as 'traditional' by both teachers and learners.

✘ It is difficult to do group work with the desks set out this way.

✘ There is a tendency for the teacher to overlook learners at the ends of each row, because they are out of the line of sight.

✘ This set-up favours the 'chalk-and-talk' method of teaching, so it can tempt you to lecture a class for longer than is useful.

✘ When moving around the class, the teacher can only work with one pair of learners at a time.

The desks in groups

Advantages

✔ Encourages a more 'modern' teaching style.

✔ Exploration and group work can happen more easily.

✔ The activities are likely to be more learner based/learner led.

✔ The teacher can talk to a whole group at a time.

✔ It is likely that they will move more freely around the room during the lesson.

Disadvantages

✘ It can be harder to control behaviour.

✘ If the teacher can't see all the faces, the learners can get away with chatting and plotting poor behaviour more easily.

✘ It can be harder for the learners to see the board.

✘ The learners may view the teacher as less traditional/strict.

✘ This perception could potentially lead to behaviour problems.

A useful alternative to the two layouts described above, is to put your desks in a U shape. This layout maximises the advantages of both rows and desks – you can see all the faces, but the learners can talk to each other more easily. Unfortunately, a U shape arrangement is usually only possible with small class sizes.

Some thoughts on different spaces

Teachers work in an array of different spaces, depending on the age range they teach and the subjects in which they specialise. Each of these spaces has its own natural advantages and disadvantages when it comes to managing behaviour. Make sure that you:

- are aware of the positive and negative aspects of your space
- consider how to maximise your control over behaviour within the space
- take steps to exploit the advantages of your space or spaces
- look for ways to minimise any difficulties you might encounter.

On the following pages you'll find a description of different types of teaching spaces, thoughts on their advantages and disadvantages in relation to behaviour, and some top tips on utilising each space to its potential.

The classroom

With its fairly fixed arrangement of seating and desks, the classroom is the classic teaching space that we all know from our own school days.

Upsides

- ✔ The desks/chairs give a sense of control and order.
- ✔ The learners sit in one place (in theory) so are easier to manage.
- ✔ There is less opportunity for physical disruptions from learners.
- ✔ The teacher can usually see all the faces when they're addressing the class.

Downsides

- ✘ The learners may feel physically restricted, and look for alternative outlets for their energy, particularly if they are restless or lack self-discipline.
- ✘ Some learners may rock back on chairs or communicate across the room to a friend.
- ✘ Learners who find it difficult to sit still might get up and wander around the room.
- ✘ If the room is small it can feel cramped with desks/chairs filling the space.

Top tips for managing behaviour in this space

- Make it a priority to keep learners in their seats.

- Have 'stay seated at all times' as a key rule.

- Train your learners to raise their hands and wait for you to come if they need help.

- Talk about *how* you want your learners to sit – teach appropriate 'sitting behaviour' and encourage good posture.

- When addressing the class, ensure all faces are turned to you, with learners attentive and ready to listen.

- For restless individuals, use 'staying in your seat' as a target, with rewards for achieving this.

- Offer outlets for physical energy: both something to 'fidget with' and an active teaching style.

- Consider incorporating a 'movement' time during sessions, for instance, just standing and stretching for a few minutes can really help with concentration.

- Don't be afraid to move desks and chairs around to adapt the layout.

- Some schools now have standing desks available, to support children's physical development and keep them more physically active, so you could explore whether this is an option.

The Foundation Stage space

This might be a unit, a purpose-built nursery or a community hall. It's typically an open space, with zoned spaces for different areas of learning. There are lots of resources and toys. The children probably have access to an outdoor space.

Upsides

- ✔ Because there are fewer desks and chairs, early years spaces often feel open and spacious.

- ✔ The children can work at different levels, sometimes on a carpet, sometimes at a desk, sometimes standing up.

- ✔ The children can move quite freely around the space, accessing resources as they wish.

- ✔ Practitioners can create a bright, colourful space for their children.

- ✔ If there's purpose-built accommodation and furniture, storage and organisation within the space is made simpler.

Downsides

✗ Because the space is more open than a classroom, there is the danger that children will move uncontrolled around the space.

✗ The practitioner needs to carefully consider all the potential risks to the children within the space.

✗ With child-initiated learning, the practitioner needs to keep an overview of the space, so they know what all the children are doing at any one time.

✗ Because there are lots of resources on offer, there's a danger that these will get messed up by learners.

Top tips for managing behaviour in this space

• Use furniture and equipment to define the space and control behaviour. For instance, you could add a table and chairs to block an area where the children tend to run.

• Ensure there aren't any hidden spots where you might lose sight of the children.

• Keep a count of the overall number of children within the setting, and do regular headcounts.

• Have a clear policy about where staff should be positioned, particularly if you free-flow between inside and outside.

• Take good care of resources, and ask that the children get involved in tidying and sorting them.

Sometimes a simple change to your use of the space can really support better behaviour. For instance, in our early years setting, we changed from having a rug for children to sit on to using rectangular carpet samples where they have their 'own' mats. This simple change resolves many of the issues around inappropriate carpet time behaviours where children annoy each other when they're sitting too close together.

The science lab

This space has fixed benches, high stools and a fixed teacher's desk at the front. There are cupboards for storing materials/equipment.

Upsides

✔ A lab can be a fun, exciting place for learners to work. The learning is often hands on and practical.

✔ There's interesting equipment to work with, and fascinating experiments to try.

✔ At secondary level, a science teacher often has the services of a departmental technician to help set up equipment.

✔ With fixed benches, learners can't create disruption by moving furniture around.

✔ With learners facing the front, it's easier for the teacher to oversee practicals.

Downsides

✗ It's harder to do group work in a lab with fixed furniture.

✗ With gas taps, Bunsen burners, etc. there are lots of opportunities for the learners to mess around.

✗ Any inappropriate behaviour could be very dangerous.

Top tips for managing behaviour in this space

• Try not to shy away from practical work if you teach in a lab. This is the type of activity that learners really enjoy.

• Teach your learners how to conduct experiments in a safe and sensible way.

• Be willing to suffer a few stressful practical lessons before they are properly trained.

• At the same time, don't put them in danger. If they refuse to behave, then remove the privilege of doing a practical.

• Make sure your class is facing the front, looking at you, and concentrating fully, before you address them.

• Talk through safety rules fully, and refer back to them regularly.

• Use 'being able to do practicals' as a reward for appropriate behaviour and maintaining attention.

• Keep temptation away from learners as far as you can.

• Make it clear right from the start that you will not stand for learners messing around with gas taps and Bunsen burners.

'Open' spaces

Your 'open' space might be a drama studio, a gym, a hall; it could have equipment or a raised stage area. Some newer schools and colleges have been designed so that these open areas can easily be created where needed.

Upsides

- ✔ This is a wonderful, spacious environment for learning.
- ✔ Your learners have a greater degree of freedom to move around.
- ✔ They are less likely to feel restricted or restless.
- ✔ Lessons in open spaces are often those subjects that learners enjoy.
- ✔ Typically, there's less focus on writing and books, and more on physical expression.

Downsides

- ✘ The sight of a big, open space may be just too tempting – your learners may be unable to resist the urge to run around.
- ✘ It can be difficult to pull the class back together into one part of the space.
- ✘ There may be high levels of noise during the lesson, making it difficult for the teacher to regain the learners' attention.
- ✘ If the teacher wants to do written work, it can be tricky to organise chairs, desks and materials.
- ✘ Learners may resent being asked to write in practical subjects, because they don't view them as involving written work.

Top tips for managing behaviour in this space

- From the first time you meet your learners in an open space, make it clear that the learning will be exciting.
- However, be clear that you have high expectations of behaviour and self-discipline. Talk about how this links to the subject – the discipline of being an actor for drama, the need for team discipline in sports for PE.
- If possible, line the learners up before they enter the space, checking in with them as they enter and reinforcing any rules about clothing, such as 'shoes off'.
- Have a 'gathering position', such as a circle, for whole-class teaching and taking the register.
- Use clipboards to do written work, booking the class into an empty classroom to write, or doing these activities for homework.
- Agree a 'silence command' for when you need the whole class's attention. Get learners to practise responding quickly to your signal.

The outdoors

Your outdoor space might be a Tarmac playground, a grassy field, a garden, a nature area or a forest school environment. You could have access to fixed equipment, such as climbing frames, or areas for different sports. Some lucky settings even have a farm or an allotment.

Upsides

✔ There's a wonderful sense of freedom, openness and light. It's great to breathe in the fresh air.

✔ The learners are freed up from the confines of the typical indoor learning space.

✔ You can explore the natural environment, and make fascinating discoveries.

✔ You can make a mess without worrying – young children particularly love getting wet and muddy!

Downsides

✘ The weather might not be great, and learning could be less than comfortable.

✘ If it is wet or cold, your learners may complain.

✘ If you have to teach outside, you might not be too happy when it's inclement weather.

✘ The learners can view being outdoors as a chance to let off steam and mess around.

✘ In an open space, it's harder to project your voice so that learners can hear.

Top tips for managing behaviour in this space

• If you are normally based in a classroom, move your learners outside to re-energise and inspire them.

• *Before* you head outside, make it clear what the rules are, and what will happen if the learners do not follow them.

• Agree a 'silence command', so that you can get your learners' attention when you need to, without having to shout.

• If the learners mess around, or behave in a dangerous way, be clear that you will take them back inside immediately.

• With younger learners, keep a constant check on numbers.

• Do a headcount before you go outside, and again when you go back in.

The teacher within the space

The way that you use your teaching space can help you achieve control of behaviour. Your learners look at the way you set up the room, and how you move around within it, to help them decide how to behave. Find ways to:

- mark the space as your territory
- make the learners feel welcome
- show that you're in overall charge
- show that positive, interesting things will happen here.

Mark the space as your territory

- Meet your learners outside the space – greet them on your terms, not on theirs.
- Create a physical barrier between the class and the room, by positioning yourself in front of the door.
- Ensure appropriate behaviour before you allow them into the room, making your expectations clear and praising those who are following them.

Make the learners feel welcome

- As you allow the learners in, greet them in a positive manner.
- Smile and look happy to see them.
- Use first names as soon as you know them.

Show that you're in charge now

- If another teacher was here previously, give clear visual indicators that the space is now yours: a striking display or a change in layout.
- Don't get stuck at the front: move around the space in a dynamic way. Visit all the learners during the course of the lesson.
- Occasionally change the layout of the room – an element of surprise keeps a class on its toes. Warn the class ahead about this if you have any learners who might struggle with a change in routine.
- It can work well to adapt the layout for the beginning of a new term, to create a 'fresh start' feel.

Show that positive, interesting things will happen in your space

- Sometimes, use the space in an unusual way. Sit on your desk or stand at the back of the room to read a piece of text.
- Use vertical space as well as horizontal – up and down as well as side to side. Crouch beside learners to chat, sit them on the floor for a story, or stand on a desk to declaim a poem.

Dealing with problem spaces

Teachers sometimes have to deal with a 'problem space' – one that is so difficult to work in that it affects the behaviour of their learners. You might teach in an old, rundown school where the paint is peeling off the classroom walls. You could have to cope with a gym that is split into two for PE lessons, with only a flimsy partition to separate you from the other class and the noise that they are making. Your room might have a huge bank of windows on one wall, making it freezing cold over the winter and boiling hot in the summer months.

My first-ever secondary classroom was the classic 'problem space'. The room was tiny, and I had some large classes who would fill the space to bursting point. There were doors at either end of the classroom, and because the room linked two areas of the school together, it was seen as a useful corridor. The room was so long and narrow that some of the learners had difficulty seeing the board. There was no room for movement once the classroom was full. The room would become progressively hotter as lessons wore on, particularly on summer afternoons when the sun shone straight into the room through windows without any blinds.

Unfortunately, you may be 'stuck' with a problem space, for a whole year or even longer. Use the following advice to help you minimise the issues you face.

In a noisy space

- Find ways to reduce the overall noise level of your lessons.
- Keep your teaching voice low and controlled, encouraging your learners to stay quiet to hear you.
- Use a silence signal to get whole-class attention, choosing one that involves minimal noise, such as raising a hand.
- Encourage learners to manage their own noise levels, for instance, having a 'noise monitor' or creating a 'noise-o-meter'.
- Divide your lessons into 'noisy' and 'quiet' times. Follow periods of noisy group work with time for quiet reflection.

- Have 'time-outs' from noise: periods when the class must work in complete silence for ten minutes or so.

In a very hot or cold space

- Check that the space meets the legal minimum temperature for the work place.
- In a very hot space, your leadership team has a duty to supply you with fans or other ways to cool it down. Ask, if they don't offer.
- Don't suffer in silence – get the health and safety or union representative involved.
- If sunlight is an issue, ask that blinds be fitted.
- Be aware of how heat can affect your mood, and the motivation levels of your learners.
- Dress appropriately for the temperature, and encourage learners to do the same, flexing the rules on uniform if necessary.

In a very cramped space

- Consider the overall layout and try experimenting with alternatives.
- Do this at the start of the year, before your learners arrive.
- A paper plan can help you to explore the options without having to move all the furniture.
- Experiment with putting your desks in groups rather than rows: this generally takes up less space.
- Consider whether turning the seating to face another way would improve things.
- Ask for shelves to be put up on the walls, so you can store paperwork without taking up more floor space.
- Find ways to take your learners out of the space to work, for instance, to the playground, hall, library or an IT suite.

Chapter 10
The Setting

The setting and behaviour

There are many reasons why learners behave inappropriately – usually completely unrelated to your skill as a teacher. Schools, colleges, early years settings and other places where education happens are a very particular kind of environment: one that can encourage appropriate behaviour or lead learners to see inappropriate behaviours as acceptable. If you work in a school or setting with a strong, positive ethos, this will contribute to the behaviours you get in your classroom. If you work in a school or setting where behaviour is a problem throughout, you might blame yourself when external factors are at least partly at fault.

Develop an awareness of all the factors governing your learners' behaviour, as listed below, so that you're less likely to get stressed and defensive if they mess around. Take steps to minimise any negative effects and try to be a part of changing the situation at your workplace for the better.

The influence of the buildings

As noted in the last chapter, our surroundings have a strong impact on the way we feel and behave. In schools and other settings, this can turn into a vicious cycle (see figure below on page 144):

If you find yourself in this situation:

- Make your classroom a sanctuary for your learners – with plants, music, lovely scents.
- Put up colourful displays, so that as soon as they walk in, they are encouraged into a positive frame of mind.
- Refuse to give up – if someone rips down a display, stick it together and put it back up again.
- Organise a group of volunteers to brighten up one area of the setting.

- Create a new garden or nature area outside, to show what can be done with a little effort.
- Don't let an overall negative atmosphere pull you into negativity. Be the shining light, leading the way with your positive aura.

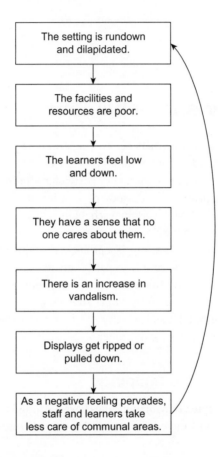

The influence of the ethos

The overall 'ethos' of your setting will have a strong impact on behaviour in your classroom. Ethos is a tricky concept to define, because it's about the 'feel' of the place. It basically refers to the prevailing culture, the way that the learners perceive the place where they are educated.

With a positive ethos:

- ✔ The learners behave appropriately, in lessons and around the school.
- ✔ There is a culture of hard work and self-discipline.
- ✔ Working hard is viewed as a positive, not a negative, thing.

✔ When new learners arrive, they pick up on this culture.

✔ There are lots of positive role models – both staff and learners.

✔ There are more likely to be lots of hard-working learners in the class.

✔ Staff have the time and energy to support individuals.

✔ Learners and staff feel happy and positive about being there.

✔ Staff stay in post longer, which in turn leads to better continuity.

With a negative ethos:

✘ A culture of poor discipline prevails.

✘ Negative attitudes to learning win out over positive ones.

✘ The 'sheer weight of numbers' makes it hard for staff to control behaviour.

✘ There is a lack of positive role models to lead change.

✘ When new learners arrive, they quickly pick up on the chaotic atmosphere.

✘ Teachers feel negative about their work and are likely not to stay in post very long.

✘ This in turn leads to learners feeling that the teachers 'don't care' and consequently playing up for new staff.

Unfortunately, once the ethos of a school becomes negative, it can take years of work to put things right. As an individual there are some steps you can take to help change the ethos of your school or setting. Turn your teaching space into a place where the negative ethos cannot penetrate, and in turn you will contribute in a small but crucial way to the slow process of change.

If lack of continuity of staff is a big problem at your school, you can make a difference simply by staying in the post for a time. This is tough in a school with a negative ethos: it will be a daily struggle against negative attitudes and the stress caused by difficult behaviour. You have to make a decision for yourself, about whether you are willing to push on through to 'make a difference' or not. Don't feel guilty if you can't, but if you are willing, remember that your choice will have a big impact on your learners.

The influence of the leadership team

The way that a school or setting is led or run has a significant impact on the behaviour you experience in lessons. The ideal is for staff and learners to see:

- a strong leadership team, who work closely together
- a keen focus on supporting and developing staff
- plenty of support for new teachers

- a sense that staff are highly valued
- backup and support for your work in the classroom
- a commitment to follow through on behaviour
- a consistent approach to the application of consequences
- a level playing field for all – not one rule for teachers and another for senior leaders
- leaders who are highly visible around the buildings.

Unfortunately, for the average teacher, there's not much to be done when the leadership is ineffective. Essentially, most teachers choose to either:

- put up with them, and have a good moan in the staffroom when they're not there
- become a 'thorn in the side', making a fuss about what isn't working and generally irritating them
- leave a school or setting, because the leadership is weak
- go for promotion, on the basis of 'if you can't beat 'em, join 'em'.

Effective behaviour policies

An effective and well thought-out behaviour policy is an invaluable aid in helping you to control behaviour in your classroom. Different settings face different kinds of behavioural issues, depending on the age and type of learners. To work well, the policy must take account of the particular situation you are in. A good policy will offer you:

- lots of motivational rewards
- a number of potential consequence levels to work with
- an 'ultimate consequence' for crisis situations
- a system of backup beyond the classroom
- effective methods of support for learners with SEND
- a way of 'keeping tabs' on the overall behaviour of an individual (particularly within a secondary school or college, where they might be in lessons with a variety of different members of staff).

To be really effective, your policy should:

- be created in conjunction with those staff working *in the classroom*, and include the views of non-teaching staff as well

- give a feeling of ownership to those people who have to use it, rather than being written by someone else and then handed over
- undergo a continuous process of review and change, reflecting the fact that the population of the setting changes over time, and therefore so must the policies
- be consistently applied, so that learners know what to expect if they behave inappropriately *whoever the member of staff is*
- have clear rules, clear consequences, and an emphasis on the positive.
- Be realistic in what your policy asks you to achieve. Consistency often falls down when leaders are over-ambitious in what they ask staff to achieve. For every school rule they ask staff to impose, leaders should consider *why you want your staff to do this and whether it is worth the effort involved in terms of learning.* For instance, if insisting on learners wearing ties is going to create conflict for staff, you could always have a uniform without a tie.
- Involve the learners too. Often, policies seem to be written without thinking about the learners who are going to be asked to follow the rules. You can involve your learners in helping decide how the policy should work, perhaps by using school council representatives to put forward learner views.

It is standard these days for learners (and their parents or carers) to be asked to agree to abide by the policy of the setting, by signing a home/school contract. However, this needs to be more than a paper exercise to really be effective. It's a great idea for the teacher to have a behaviour contract that all the learners sign: this can be displayed on the classroom wall.

Below is a description of a typical whole-school behaviour policy, to show you how and why it might be effective. If you feel that your school behaviour policy is not working well, you might like to suggest including some of the following ideas to help improve it. You will usually have the opportunity to do this through the meetings structure in your school.

The 'rules' or 'code of conduct'

You might have two sets of rules to work with – a set within your behaviour policy, and a second set for your individual classroom. The first set outlines general behaviours expected around the school, the second is that list of specific expectations that you share with your learners in the first lesson. The rules in your policy might refer to:

- how learners should work
- what behaviour is expected in the classroom

- what behaviour is expected around the buildings
- how staff and learners should behave towards each other
- how the environment and the equipment should be treated
- which behaviours are unacceptable, and the consequences of doing these things.

The way that rules are phrased varies widely according to the age of the learners.

Put a laminated set of rules on your wall to refer to as you reward and reprimand your learners. A good set of rules will:

- be short, clear and simply worded
- be phrased in a positive ('do this') rather than a negative ('don't do this') way
- give a sense of teamwork – 'we' rather than 'you'
- make the teacher's life easier, so they can get on with teaching
- not involve petty expectations or be unrealistic to achieve.

Motivators and consequences

As a first port of call, the policy should include a range of positive motivators for staff to use with the learners. There should be a list of the available rewards used across the school, but it can also be really helpful to list some positive strategies that teachers can use, before they move on to apply consequences. (For instance, move closer to the learner, use 'proximity praise' to highlight the positive things someone *close* to the learner is doing, and so on.)

Within the policy, there should also be a system of consequences that build up gradually. Typically, with the youngest children, the consequences will not be punitive, but will involve discussions and restorative conversations about what happened, how it can be resolved, and how the situation might be handled better in the future. This might build up to asking parents or carers to come in to talk with staff about the problems, and perhaps a young child being given an individualised behaviour plan, with targets and rewards.

In schools, and for older learners, the list of consequences might involve:

- a verbal warning
- a written warning
- a short consequence
- a longer or more serious consequence
- a referral to senior staff.

With a gradual build-up of consequences, the teacher can maintain control and avoid confrontation. There should be chances for the learner to decide to cooperate, but the consequences should not take too long to apply. It's important that these graduated levels are used consistently across the setting, or learners get mixed messages. Those staff who do apply the policy consistently should not be seen as overly strict or unfair.

The 'ultimate' consequence

Schools will also have an 'ultimate' consequence, whereby a situation that has gone out of control can be retrieved, usually by removing the learner from the classroom. It could be that a learner is becoming physically violent, or simply that the teacher cannot continue teaching if the learner remains in the room.

In these instances, there would normally be a senior teacher available to come and remove the learner. The class teacher typically sends for help by using a 'red card', a special slip, or by summoning help through an 'on call' system. Unfortunately, it can be the case that teachers send for help and no one turns up, particularly in schools with a lot of behavioural issues happening simultaneously, which unfortunately undermines both the teacher and the power of the consequence.

The ultimate consequence offers a 'fallback' position for when behaviour becomes completely unacceptable or dangerous to the teacher and other learners. It should not be used as a way of repeatedly removing tricky learners from the classroom. For this to be effective, the teacher must not feel worried about how other staff will perceive them if they use it. Equally, though, it must only be used when it is really necessary.

Behaviour units and pupil referral units

Many secondary schools now provide a specialist on-site unit where learners whose behaviour is very challenging in a mainstream classroom can be taught for periods of time. Referrals can be part of a system of consequences; for instance, when a learner reaches a certain point in the disciplinary policy, this could result in time spent in the behaviour unit or isolation area.

These units should be staffed by teachers experienced in dealing with children who have social, emotional and mental health issues. The unit should have a high teacher-to-learner ratio, so that individual attention is given to each learner's needs. The eventual aim of time spent in a referral unit is to reintegrate the learner back into the classroom, rather than to keep them tucked away in what used to be termed a 'sin bin'.

Restorative approaches

Restorative approaches (also referred to as 'restorative justice') offer an alternative way of thinking about handling behaviour for both teachers and schools. The idea behind the approach is to focus on building and repairing relationships, rather than using punitive methods to get children to conform to the rules. Although doing this requires more effort and time, it can be effective in *changing* behaviour, as well as just managing it. Using a restorative approach is time consuming, and staff must be well trained in the methods to get it right. However, when I have spoken to teachers whose schools do use this approach to handling behaviour, they feel strongly that it is an effective and valuable idea.

Even if your setting does not use restorative approaches at an institutional level, there is no reason why you cannot incorporate some of the ideas at classroom level. Many of the methods that I outline in this book are about building relationships, and thinking through behaviours, as well as about managing them. At classroom level:

- Find ways to boost relationships within your classroom, and beyond: both teacher/learner relationships and those between learners.
- Where possible, take the time to talk with a learner after the event, about why the problem behaviour happened. If you have had to put a learner in a detention, this can be a useful time to talk things over.
- Don't be afraid to tell a learner how their behaviour makes you and the other learners feel, and to talk about their own feelings as well. What were they feeling when they behaved in this way? Is there something you could all do to avoid it happening again in the future?
- Aim to encourage a sense of empathy, and an openness in talking about how our emotions affect our behaviour.
- Aim to help all learners feel like part of the 'community', whether the school as a whole, the class or peer group. Help them to restore their position within the community when things go wrong.
- Use the language of choice, to encourage learners to see their behaviour as their responsibility and to understand that they have agency over their behaviours.
- When you do have to use a consequence, remember to use language that makes it clear that it is the behaviour that is a problem, rather than the learner.

Effective support systems

When you have difficulties in controlling behaviour, what you most need are good support systems: someone you trust enough to share your worries with, or someone who can give you specialist advice on an issue. By its very nature, teaching is usually a fairly solitary occupation: working in your classroom you have little idea about what is going on elsewhere in the school. It is easy for the imagination to run riot, and to start thinking that all the other staff have perfect behaviour in their classrooms, to imagine that it is only you who can't 'get your class to behave'. Difficult and challenging behaviours can make you feel upset and alone; with an effective support system in place, you always have someone to turn to when in need.

Other teachers/staff

Teachers often develop strong bonds with their colleagues, at least partly because the job is so physically and emotionally taxing. The tougher the school or setting, often the stronger the bonds between staff. Find time to go to the staffroom during the day if at all possible. Other teachers can support you by:

- being there for you to 'let off steam' and have a moan
- giving you tips, advice and strategies
- helping you maintain a sense of perspective
- understanding what you're going through
- suggesting something that works with a particular individual.

Support staff

Increasingly, there are members of staff other than the teacher within a classroom. Although their key role is to support learning, inevitably, as part of this, they can help you manage behaviour as well. Perhaps the best use of support staff's time is in helping those learners whose learning needs lead to issues with behaviour. If a learner messes around when they struggle to understand an activity, get your teaching assistant to help them access the learning as a priority.

Special educational needs staff

The special educational needs staff within your setting should be an invaluable resource for you when dealing with difficult behaviour. They have specialist knowledge about the problems you are experiencing, and will be aware of some of the background factors that can cause the behaviours you face. Get to know these members of staff and approach them for information and advice.

Leaders

Some leaders are a helpful source of comfort and even inspiration. As with any staff in a school, though, the truth is that some are effective and others less so. Staff in a leadership position will at least have a few years' experience. If you are relatively inexperienced, they can advise you because they've probably already encountered many of the same problems when they were in the classroom fulltime. Staff in leadership positions have a certain level of authority with learners, by virtue of their position in the hierarchy. Hopefully they can use this authority to help you manage behaviour. For instance, a head of department could say, in front of the class, that you can refer any particularly troublesome learners to them.

Parents and carers

Most parents and carers are genuinely keen and willing to support the work that teachers do with their children. Often, though, they don't have a clear idea of how to go about doing this, or a full understanding of what their child is actually doing in your classroom. If an individual causes you ongoing problems, talk to their parents or carers about what's going on. Sometimes, parents are completely unaware of exactly what their children are doing at school. (After all, how many learners confess their inappropriate behaviour when they arrive home?) This is especially important at secondary and post-compulsory levels, where there is relatively little contact between the setting and the home.

Of course, it could be that the parents or carers of your most difficult learners are part of the problem, rather than a potential part of the solution. Check with senior staff before getting in touch with the home, to ensure you are aware of any child protection issues.

To encourage parents to support the work you do with your learners:

- Give them information about what goes on in your classroom.
- Invite them in to see what your learners have achieved.
- Let them know how they can support learning at home.
- Explain the kind of volunteer tasks they can do to assist you.

Teaching unions

Your union representative can be an excellent source of support, particularly if you are facing severe issues with behaviour. There may be health and safety concerns involved. There might also be accusations flying around from disgruntled learners, when you challenge their inappropriate behaviour. If a learner does make a complaint, get advice from your union representative about your legal position and your rights.

Chapter 11

Supporting Behaviour: Early Years and Primary (3–11)

Young children's behaviour

Although the vast majority of the advice I give in this book applies to learners of all ages, there are strategies which are best suited to handling the behaviour of learners at specific stages in their school life. In this chapter, you'll find tips and techniques for those of you who work in the early years or primary sector (3–11 years old).

Please note: in this chapter, because I'm dealing only with the youngest part of the age range, I use the term children rather than learners.

Some key principles apply when working with young children:

- Remember that an early years setting or primary school may feel like a confusing and even frightening place for children at first.

- Very young children are still closely attached to their parents or carers; building confidence and independence is key at this stage.

- Young children are very much at the beginning of learning personal, social and emotional skills, such as empathy, impulse control and managing their emotions. For the early years practitioner, helping them develop these skills is as important as subject learning.

- Just as you teach subjects to children, so we can support them to build and develop their self-regulation skills. This will happen through all of the interactions that you have with your children. Use the process of co-regulation (working alongside the child to support their impulse control) in order to build self-regulation.

- At this stage, the pattern for the rest of the child's educational career is being set, so it's crucial to get it right.

- This is an opportunity to set positive learning and behaviour habits, patterns and routines, rather than negative ones.

- The ideal is to model appropriate behaviour, give clear boundaries and offer plenty of praise and support.

- We should never scare young children into behaving well, but aim to encourage them by using positive approaches. Bear in mind that young children might view the adults differently to how those adults think they are being perceived.

- Any interventions and support given now is likely to have a much greater impact than those made later on.

- The practitioner or teacher spends much more time with the same group of children, and can build a very close relationship with them.

- For some children, the early years or primary teacher may be the first adult to model appropriate behaviour.

- A child who has never been taught about boundaries may take time to settle into the routines of the setting.

Starting out: early years settings

In private, voluntary and independent early years settings, children often arrive in dribs and drabs, rather than in a whole 'year group' as they might in a nursery or Reception class in schools. Your first few days and weeks will be as much about getting to know an individual child, as about getting to know a whole group. Remember:

- The children will be nervous and unsure – it will take them a while to build up confidence and to settle. For many, this is their first encounter with the world outside of their home environment: work to make it a positive one.

- A home visit can be a great way to learn about a child's interests and needs, and to understand how you can support the family as well as the child.

- In the early days, your role is as much about helping children settle in, and dealing with the social and emotional aspects of their development, as it is about dealing with inappropriate behaviour. Any 'problem' behaviours will communicate what the child is thinking or feeling.

- Clear structures and routines will really help your children to settle quickly. The children need to know what happens at what point in the session, where to go if they need the toilet or what to do if they need a drink.

- If possible, it works really well to have a dedicated member of staff to support new starters. They can show the parents around and help children settle in when they first arrive. Once the children begin to settle, you can allocate them a key worker.

- Don't make assumptions about special educational needs at this stage – the children will probably be quiet, as they get to know the setting. Be on the lookout for anything that is clearly worrying or obvious, but take your time to get to know the children first.

- Those children with speech or communication difficulties or English as an additional language will find it hard to take in what is going on. They may struggle to communicate what they are feeling and thinking. Keep a special eye out for any children who have delayed speech.

- Don't assume that the children will understand everything you say to them the first time you say it.

- Make lots and lots of use of tone – you really cannot overdo it with this age group. Using lots of variations of tone will also bring life into your facial expressions, which really aids understanding for this age group.

- Get to know each child's parents and carers – at this age, close contact with parents is key to helping children learn and develop.

- Learn not to overly attend to low-level inappropriate behaviours that seem to be about seeking attention. A lot of the inappropriate behaviours you see in young children are ones designed to get an adult's attention, because the child needs something else. Train yourself to give attention for positive behaviours, and offer support, before the child feels any need to get your attention in less positive ways.

Starting out: primary school

The first few days and weeks with a primary class are crucial in setting the pattern for the year. This applies just as much to organising clear routines for behaviour as it does to encouraging proper learning habits. For the primary school teacher, who works with this one class for the whole year, it is vital to create and develop good relationships with each child right from the start. It's also vital to begin building that sense of the class as a team, working together to achieve their best.

It's tempting to spend lots of time before the school year starts doing detailed planning. This is especially so if you are new to the job. You want to get ahead of yourself and be well organised. But you've got to meet and get to know your children before you can plan effectively for them. Get a feel for the individuals, and for the group as a whole, before you dive into longer-term planning.

When you start out with your new primary class, make it a priority to gather knowledge and information about the children.

- **Talk to colleagues:** in a reception class, liaise with nursery or pre-school practitioners to find out about the children's individual needs. With classes higher up the school, talk to other members of staff who have taught these children. Get some general input, but don't make judgements based only on other people's impressions.

- **Consider special educational needs:** talk with your SENCO and other professionals, to find out about any children who have particular learning, behavioural or physical needs. Get hold of paperwork relating to the children and read it through so you know what to expect.

- **Learn the names:** the quicker you learn your children's names, the better you can support their behaviour and help them learn. Use displays, discussions, name games, sticky labels, nameplates for desks, whatever you can think of. When the children are at their desks, use a seating plan to learn names.

- **Get to know them:** rather than plunging straight into the curriculum, take time to get to know your children as individuals. Create learning activities that facilitate this, such as talking about 'my favourite things' at circle time or doing 'show and tell' sessions.

- **Set your standards now:** this is the time to lay out your stall. Be firm, fair and clear, but not overly assertive or imposing. Remember that you are effectively their main carer, beyond their home environment, and a key part of your role is that gentler side of the teacher or practitioner's role.

Clearly you don't want to scare young children into cooperating, but what you should still do is come across as clear, confident and sure of the behaviour you want. Your children will actually feel more secure, and happier, if they feel that the teacher is able to control the behaviour of their peers.

A brief guide to self-regulation

The skills that young children need to develop, in order to learn how to behave, are referred to as self-regulation skills. These encompass a range of different executive (or brain) functions which allow us to do various things. The diagram below summarises the skills that children are developing, around behaviour, when you work with them on their social and emotional development and help them build their self-regulation.

Self-regulation develops through a range of factors in early childhood, which include secure attachments, unconditional positive regard from carers, the chance for the child to have agency and learn from their mistakes, and reliable access to resources. In addition, they need to be supported to access high levels of challenge, in order to learn goal-setting behaviours and also to build their resilience.

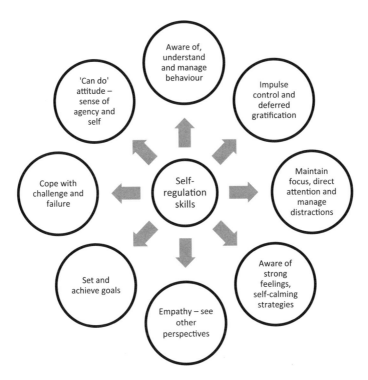

There are lots of ways in which you can support children to build their self-regulation skills in your classroom. Here are some practical suggestions:

✔ Ensure warm and responsive interactions with children, which make them feel able to take risks and face challenges.

✔ Help them to understand their emotions, by naming them, and supporting children to self-calm when they become dysregulated.

✔ Give children elements of agency within classroom routines, to show them that good choices lead to positive outcomes.

✔ Promote empathy across the curriculum, for instance, by asking questions about how characters in a story might feel.

✔ Give trust and responsibility, especially to those children who are tricky to trust – if you never trust them, they have no way to show whether or not they can be responsible.

✔ Encourage children to feel the impulse to 'go', but to hold back on responding to the feeling. Games such as 'statues' or 'grandmother's footsteps' are great for this.

Teaching learning behaviours

It's really important to remember that you're here to help the children learn, rather than to manage their behaviour. However, it's also important to remember that helping them to learn to manage their *own* behaviour is clearly one of your learning goals – this is what supporting self-regulation is all about. Help children to build the appropriate behaviours early on, so that they can maintain a focus on learning. Children are going to be in education for a long time: certain behaviours need to become automatic, so that learning can happen more easily. The younger the children, the newer these learning behaviours might be to them. Adapt the suggestions below to the age of the children you work with.

Sitting behaviour

When they're sitting down, be a bit particular about how you encourage the children to sit – whether on a carpet or a chair. On the carpet, encourage them to sit up straight, cross their legs, fold their arms, and stick to their own personal space. Be clear about why it's important for their safety not to tip back on chairs. If you want children to ask permission before getting up, set that expectation right now. At the same time, be sensible about how long you get them to sit, according to their age and the kind of setting you're working in. These sound like minor issues to worry about, but there are several very important reasons to get this aspect right:

- Proper sitting helps lead to full attention, and consequently to more effective learning.
- It can be a safety issue – tipping back on chairs is dangerous.
- It's a health issue as well – they're going to be sitting *an awful lot* over the next however many years in education. Help them learn to sit with good posture.
- There is less chance the children will annoy each other, and consequently less chance of those complaints about 'they pushed me', if they stick to their own personal space.
- You send a message about who is leading the learning in your classroom, and that you are in overall control of the teaching space.

Of course, bear in mind that young children need lots of physical activity – the younger they are, the more activity they need. Balance times when you need them to sit and pay attention, with times when they get to be active.

Listening behaviour

When you have to talk to the whole group, you want your children to be silent and attentive so they hear and understand what is being said. Exactly the same applies when one of the children is talking in a whole-group situation. Teach good listening behaviour right from the start, and you do your children a huge favour. If they learn how to listen properly, they will learn much more effectively. Use lots of eye contact and pauses, to check that you have their full attention. Ask for input from the children, to check for understanding. For instance, use talk partners to discuss a question you have asked, or get the children to repeat something you have just said.

Answering behaviour

Teach your children about what you want them to do when you ask a question. Again, this is something that will happen throughout their school life. The key learning behaviour you're after is that the children learn not to call out. The exact approach you use will depend on the kind of question you're asking, the age of the children, and also on your viewpoint about what works best for learning. You might use:

- talk partners, where the children discuss their ideas, then you ask for a response
- direct questioning of named individuals, with some thinking-time first, i.e. 'Charlotte, can you answer this question…'
- the 'hands up to answer, everyone tries to participate' approach
- a random method, such as putting names on lolly sticks and drawing these out of a pot, or using an online random name generator.

Most teachers use a mix of approaches, but you can get the habits in place from the start. Use prompts to ingrain those habits, for example, asking: 'Put up your hand if you can tell me…'

Activity behaviours

Be clear with your children about exactly how they should approach activities around learning, whether group work, discussions, writing tasks, tidying-up time, and so on. With older children you might put a list up on the wall, or in the front of exercise books, as a reminder. At Foundation Stage, your list might be:

- we share
- we take care of the toys

- we take turns
- we tidy up when we're finished.

With older children, your list for writing activities might be:

- put a title and date, and underline it
- write as neatly as you can
- take time to check your spelling and punctuation
- work quietly (or in silence if you prefer)
- put your hand up if you have a question or if you need help.

To get these learning behaviours in place, you need to repeat them over and over again with your children, until they become habits. You also need to insist on what you've asked for: just as with your expectations, you must model them consistently. Once you get these habits in place, your life gets easier, and you can focus on the learning.

'Training' your children

In the film *Kindergarten Cop*, Arnold Schwarzenegger trains his class of young children as though they are at 'police academy'. This fictional example demonstrates a very important point about working with young children. Train them to behave well right from the start, *and make it seem fun to behave like this*, and they will happily follow your instructions. This should leave you free to deal with the minority of children who have more complex behavioural or learning needs. Effectively, this 'training' involves sharing your expectations and letting the class see them in action.

You can 'train' your children in:

- **The morning routine:** what happens when the children arrive in the morning – what do they do first? What happens about books, equipment, packed lunches and registering? Where are you, and what are you doing at this point? At what point do they come to the carpet or settle down to an activity?

- **Responding to your signals:** ideally, you want the children to respond quickly and habitually to your signals, so it's easy to gain their attention. This isn't about being a 'control freak', but about creating a safe environment, and ensuring effective learning can take place.

- **Dealing with equipment:** train your children to collect, use and put away equipment as you want them to do it. This saves you time and effort, but more importantly, it encourages them to take responsibility for their own learning.

Spice this up by adding a bit of competition: 'Who's got the neatest drawer?' or 'Who can pick up three blocks first?'

- **The end-of-day routine:** get your children trained to tidy up, to tuck in chairs, to leave the room as they found it. This helps them learn responsibility, and shows them that the space and resources are of value, and must be treated with respect.

Behaviour management doesn't have to be a heavy and weighty thing, where you drone on at your children about how they must do this, and mustn't do that, and on and on and on. If you keep it light and use a soft touch, you can often get them to do what you want without them realising this is what you're doing. Pre-empt the typical problems you face, and aim to find a way to get a strategy in place, to prevent the problem ever arising. To make behaving well seem like fun, you could:

- **Turn tasks into a 'game':** consider the way you present tasks and activities to your children. Use vocabulary that suggests fun and challenge rather than boredom and hard work. For instance, to get a group to lie down and be still for story time, introduce a game of 'sleeping lions'. The children must pretend to be lions, fast asleep and very still.

- **Enter the world of make-believe:** children of all ages respond to make-believe (and, indeed, so do older learners as well). They love the chance to use their imaginations: the opportunity to be someone, something or somewhere they are not. For example, to get a group to tidy up the room very quietly, tell them to pretend that there's a sleeping giant beneath the floor, and they really mustn't wake him. (Particularly effective if you've just been reading *Jack and the Beanstalk*).

- **Treat them as adults:** another very useful fiction is that the children are much more grown up than they really are. For instance, they could play the part of a science professor while doing an experiment. Foundation Stage practitioners can have great fun with this, getting the children to be firefighters, doctors, animal-rescue workers, circus performers – the possibilities are limitless. When you get your children to take on the role of an expert, you can use it to encourage responsible behaviour and attitudes. Interact with the children as though they are adults, expressing surprise at any silliness: 'I can hardly believe you're doing that, Professor Smith, seeing as you're a world-famous scientist.'

Seven key strategies for success

Here are seven key strategies and approaches that are particularly useful in the early years and at primary school.

1 Know how to get your children's attention

With young children it's important to find effective ways to get their attention, and to get it quickly if needed. The younger the children, the more easily distracted they are, and consequently the harder it can be to gain everyone's attention. In an early years setting, many of the traditional structures of a classroom do not apply (children at desks, doing activities set by the teacher). There's less sense of control, but there will still be times when you need to pull everyone together.

Your children might be:

- totally engrossed in an activity
- about to do something dangerous
- getting overexcited or too loud
- moving between activities
- in the middle of a noisy discussion task.

When you need to get your children's attention, you want to avoid shouting because it stresses your voice, suggests a loss of control and, anyway, is not easily heard in a noisy room. Set up a 'silence signal' with your group – a signal agreed ahead of time, that tells them 'I need silence now'. Bear in mind that it doesn't have to be the teacher giving the silence signal – in our setting, one of the children rings a handbell to bring the group together first thing in the morning.

There are lots of different techniques you can use:

- **The non-verbal signal:** this is effective because it doesn't add any noise to the setting. The children fall silent without hearing anything, so it gives a sense that the teacher is in control of the situation. Your non-verbal signal might be a 'silent seat', where you sit when you want the children to come straight to the carpet. You could raise a hand to indicate that the children should stop what they are doing, fall silent and raise their hands too.

- **The time target:** this is a useful technique for older children, because it places the responsibility on them, rather than on you. Before they start an activity, set them a challenge: while they work they must keep an eye on the clock, and at a specified time they should fall silent in preparation for the next instruction. At the appointed time you will usually find one or two of your more observant individuals 'shushing' the rest of the class for you.

- **The visual signal:** this one's great for shorter activities. Get hold of a large egg timer, or download a stopwatch on to your interactive whiteboard. When you say 'go', the children start work; when the sand or timer runs out, they must stop.

- **The targeted command:** for this signal, you do a countdown, for instance, 'Five, four, three, two, one, freeze!' On 'freeze', the children must freeze as still as statues. Make it into a 'game' – get your children to respond more quickly each time you play the game.

- **The sound signal:** you play a brief burst of music, give a quick whistle, ring a bell, or any other kind of interesting sound. This indicates that it's time for the children to stop what they're doing and pay attention. Praise those learners who stop quickest to encourage a faster response next time round.

- **'We all join in':** start clicking your fingers in a pattern, for instance, two slow clicks followed by three fast ones. The children must join in with your pattern. Because they are concentrating on copying your rhythm, they will probably stop talking. You can then slow down your clicking gradually, until the children all stop at the same moment.

2 Understand how to keep your children's attention

Because young children are so easily distracted, you should work hard to keep the attention of your children once you've got it. This is particularly so when you're explaining an activity or doing a teacher-led task. The older the children, the longer the stretches they will be able to concentrate for and pay attention. You'll also need to ensure that they focus their attention on activities during the course of the lesson.

To achieve this key strategy:

- **Keep eye contact:** as you talk to your children, keep your eyes moving around to ensure that every child is focused. If you notice someone is not, pause for a moment, without saying anything. The child should pick up on the fact that you have stopped speaking and look at you to find you looking back at them. Don't be afraid to pause as often as is needed to ensure attention.

- **Repeat back to me:** when you explain an activity, it's easy for children to look as though they're listening when in fact the words are not actually registering in their brains. After you've finished your run-through of what you want the children to do, get someone to repeat this back to you. With older children, choose a child who you suspect was not really listening. Clarify any possible misunderstandings before the children begin work.

- **Chunk up your sessions:** break up longer lessons or sessions into smaller chunks, to keep your children focused. In the Foundation Stage, you could have whole-group times, times for free choice, times for a focused activity, perhaps with a targeted group. When you offer breaks between activities, use this as a chance for the children to 'stretch' themselves: this could be a quick 'brain stretch' (perhaps some mental maths games) or a physical stretch (such as shaking out their bodies).

3 Learn how to give clear instructions

There will be lots of times during your day when you need to give instructions to the group or class. It could be learning related (how to complete an activity); it could be about your routine (time to wash your hands for a snack). It is hard for young children to take in all the things that are going on around them. After all, only recently their parents or carers were their whole world. Now they are in an early years setting or school, where many different things are going on. It's easy for them to get sidetracked.

One of the main causes of what we call inappropriate behaviour is a child *who doesn't understand what you want them to do*. They're not intentionally being difficult, it's just that they don't actually understand, so they can't complete the task or activity you've set. It's surprisingly hard to give good instructions: if you're new to the profession, don't worry if you're finding it hard – it's a skill that comes with lots of practice.

In fact, understanding instructions seems to be an area where even adults have a 'blind spot'. When I set up an activity at a training day, I aim to give very clear instructions about the task (and obviously I'm experienced at doing this). Even so, I joke that when I set the group off on the activity, someone in the room will say to their group, 'What were we meant to do again?'

If the children don't understand your instructions, all sorts of disruptions can arise. You set them off on an activity, only to find that five hands immediately go up, with children saying 'I don't understand what I'm meant to do'. You then have to stop everyone and explain the task over again. Those children who are not confident enough to ask for help might mess around to cover up their lack of understanding.

Overcome these issues by giving effective instructions in the first place, using the following strategies and approaches to help you:

- **Be clear, simple and direct:** make your instructions as simple as possible – aim them at the weakest, most confused child in the class. Speak with a slow, well-modulated voice, emphasising key words as you talk.

- **Give a visual backup:** some children find it much easier to understand what they see than what they hear, particularly if they are new to English or their language development is delayed. Use lots of visual methods to reinforce your instructions – hand signals, diagrams, icons, key points written on the board, props, etc.

- **Give an example or a demonstration:** go through examples with the children to reinforce what you want them to do. An example helps us take an idea from the abstract concept to a more concrete understanding of that concept. Ask for volunteers to help you demonstrate – this helps you to encourage participation and check for understanding.

- **Consider your language:** as adults, we use words freely, without considering the need for understanding. For young children, with a limited vocabulary, ensure that every word is easily understood. Be as specific and explicit as you can about what you need. For instance, instead of saying 'take care with your punctuation', ask your children to 'make sure you put all the full stops and commas in the right places'.

- **Use time indicators:** to avoid an aural jumble, make the timing of what you want very clear. To clarify order, use phrases such as 'first I want you to…', then 'next I need you to …' Set a clear time to complete the activity you've set.

- **Follow the 'rule of three':** young children find it hard to retain more than about three instructions at once. This is a good guide to the maximum amount of information they can process at any one time. Where possible when giving instructions, limit yourself to three main points.

- **Use lots of repetition:** train yourself to repeat instructions over and over again, in a range of clear, direct ways, to ensure you have complete understanding. Ask the children to repeat back to you what you said, to check for any areas of weak comprehension.

Here's a quick example of a teacher giving clear instructions to a Year 3 class:

> 'When I say go, I want you to go straight to your desks and open your exercise books. First, write the title and date. Then complete questions one, two and three from the board. You have ten minutes. Bilal, please could you repeat what I've just said to the class?'

When you set up an activity, get help from teaching assistants and other staff. Share information about the activities before the lesson: they can help you by explaining the activity to children who don't understand, but they can only do this if they understand the activity themselves.

4 Distraction, not reaction

The younger the children you work with, the less likely it is that you will need to turn to any of the higher-level consequences described in Chapter 6. In most instances, you should hopefully be able to use a low-level approach – non-verbal signals such as a disappointed look. With your more challenging children, you might need to use a system such as thinking time. Of course, there might be some children whose behaviour is so out of control that you have no choice but to put in place one-to-one adult support and help. But most of the time, your main focus will be on the clear setting of boundaries, rather than on the application of consequences.

When young children behave inappropriately, one of the very best approaches of all is to offer them a distraction. At this age, children are not making the kind of conscious decision to disrupt that you might experience in a secondary school or an FE college. Even your most disruptive children will have got themselves into the subconscious habit of being difficult, rather than sitting down one day and thinking, 'I really must disrupt Miss Smith's lesson.' When you 'react to' problem behaviour, you draw attention to it – you're also likely to lose the flow of what you were doing. When you 'distract from' problem behaviour, you deal with it quickly, and in a low-key manner.

Here are some examples, to show you what I mean:

For example...

Three years old

Charlie is wriggling around during 'show and tell' on the carpet.

React to: The practitioner brings attention to the problem, by saying, 'Charlie, stop wriggling around and wait your turn.'

Distract from: The practitioner signals to her colleague to take Charlie away to set out some toys for when circle time is finished.

Six years old

Grace is disrupting a whole-class carpet-time session by repeatedly digging her elbow into the person next to her.

React to: The teacher makes Grace stand up, and tells her off in front of the class.

Distract from: The teacher asks Grace to come to the front and help write something up on the whiteboard.

Nine years old

T. J. is walking around the classroom and disrupting others, even though the learners have been told to stay in their seats.

React to: The teacher goes up to T. J. and says, 'Why on earth are you out of your seat?'

Distract from: The teacher says to T. J., 'While you're up, hand out these sheets, but then *straight back to your seat, okay*? Please don't make me speak to your parents again, T.J.'

This is not to say that you shouldn't deal with a child who repeatedly behaves inappropriately, especially at the older end of this age range. If the child has already been told not to do something, and persists in doing it, you will need to turn to consequences of some kind; they just don't necessarily need to be punitive. Use the rule of thumb from the teaching styles chapter (see Chapter 5, 'An assertive style' on page 65): 'once nicely, once firmly, then get on with it'. Remember, too, that you should still talk to the child about any support you can give them – start by asking: 'What's the problem?' or 'Is there something I can do to support you?' Don't let this interrupt the flow of your teaching, but do chat after the event, when the rest of the class are on task, and you have the chance to talk in private.

5 Take an overview

When you work with one group or class for all or most of the time, it is easy to get pulled into fixed patterns of behaviour with them. You know the individuals so well, that you have specific expectations about how they will behave when you ask them to do something. For instance, the moment you set a task, you home in on that 'difficult' table of children; or, you trail around after Amelia during free play, because you know she always gets herself into trouble.

As well as helping and focusing on individuals, it's also important to keep a continuous overview of the class or group as a whole. What's happening on the other side of the room, while you're doing that craft activity with one group? What are the overall noise levels like; do you need to stop the class to pull the level of excitement down a bit? It's a tricky technique to master, because you want to sit and give individual children your attention. But eventually, with experience, you learn to develop those 'eyes in the back of your head'.

When you set the whole class off on an activity:

- Don't move towards any one group or child immediately.
- Stand still for a few moments, and gain an overview of the entire group.
- Consider: who's settling down and focusing, and who looks unsure?
- Give a positive – 'Green table's doing great! Straight on task, I see. Well done, green table!', rather than moving straight towards any children who are off task.

Similarly, when you're sitting with an individual or small group to support them:

- Keep an eye out for what's happening on the other side of the room.
- Use non-verbal signals as required to deal with any issues.
- If you do speak to the class, make sure it's to highlight someone who's working well, rather than someone who isn't.
- Have a constant feel for how loud overall noise levels are.

- Have an ongoing sense of levels of energy or conversely lack of motivation.
- Stop the class to pull the children together, or to give any reminders as and when required.

Of course, this doesn't mean that you should never give your full attention to one child or one group. Don't intervene with every tiny incident – sometimes, give yourself permission to focus fully on one of your learners.

6 Spread your attention around

If you work with a class or group where there are lots of children with behavioural difficulties, what can happen is that those children take up the majority of your time and energy. Even though you try to focus on the positive, there are so many low-level incidents of inappropriate behaviour that you simply cannot avoid getting sucked into dealing with them. In part, this is a result of inclusion – there are simply more children with complex needs in the modern-day classroom. During the pandemic, the disruption to schooling, and to children's normal routines, certainly did not help the situation either. Although this is not the place for a debate about the merits of inclusion, what it does mean is that teachers are facing more incidents of inappropriate behaviour, and often behaviour that is challenging and hard to handle.

If this is the case for you, it can start to feel like you focus only on the difficult children. You might feel as though you are giving out loads of rewards to the poorly behaved children, and none to those who always sit quietly and get on with their learning. When you're managing behaviour, it's really important to remember:

Although you should support and help the minority of children who have high levels of behavioural needs, you should try not to do so at the expense of the majority who want to learn. Don't be too hard on yourself if you don't get it right, though – it's tough.

In the day-to-day reality of the classroom, this means that you must not feel guilty about occasionally focusing totally on the learners who are really keen to get on with their work. If you are using up all your energy and time dealing with one child with really challenging behaviour, then insist that the school does something about giving you additional support. Be willing to ignore low-level inappropriate behaviour, in order to focus in on helping those children who never seem to get your attention. Alternatively, push through with the behaviour policy, and if that means sending a child to a more senior member of staff because they are constantly attacking others, then that is what you must do. Aim to spread yourself around as equally and as fairly as you can, so that all the children get the benefit of some time spent with you.

7 Get creative with rewards

In early years and primary settings, you can have great fun getting creative with rewards. Show your children that *behaving well is fun* and that *learning can be fun too*. Perhaps the very best reward of all is a lesson or activity that is enjoyable and engrossing, and where the children really feel that they've learnt something. There's little to beat the sense of achievement of working hard and seeing a creditable end result.

When I meet early years and primary teachers, I'm always amazed at how inventive they are with rewards, particularly when creating whole-class reward systems. The point with rewards is, you don't have to be consistent like you do with consequences. You can create your own unique and imaginative approaches, ones to which you know your class will respond.

Here are a few suggestions, inspired by some of the early years and primary staff I've worked with over the last few years:

- **Deputy diners:** the children earn the right to be a 'deputy diner' – each teacher nominates a child for this privilege. At lunch time, the 'deputy diners' sit and have their lunch with the deputy head. The table is set with proper linen, a vase with real flowers, proper napkins, china plates and shiny silver cutlery. They are served at their table by a 'waiter' (this could be the headteacher if you really want to have fun).

- **All the colours of the rainbow:** the teacher creates a huge 'weather' display on the wall. There are various Velcro pictures that can be attached to the display, depending on how well the children are working and behaving. The weather might be rainy, to show that the teacher is not happy, or the sun could come out, when the class is working well. If things are going brilliantly, there is the ultimate accolade of a rainbow.

- **Treasure box:** I really liked this idea and I have used it as a bit of fun when I'm training teachers. You will need to find an attractive box, ideally one with a lock and key. Fill the box with all different kinds of 'treasures'. My box has packs of pencils, little notebooks, packets of seeds, pots of glitter and sweets. When a child does something really brilliant, they get to dip in the treasure box and pick out a prize.

For a document to download, listing loads of different, creative rewards, visit my website www.suecowley.co.uk and search 'Free Downloads'.

Towards secondary school

By the time they reach the last year of the primary phase, learners are preparing to make the transition from child to young adult. They are on the cusp of becoming teenagers. But they're not yet quite ready to shrug off some of the childlike feelings and emotions which may lead to immature and silly behaviour. At this stage, the children have an added sense of confidence as a result of being 'top dogs' in the school. Things change dramatically when they arrive at secondary school, where they are once again at the bottom of the pile.

At this age, children may start to push at the boundaries and test adult authority, as they take the first steps on the road to becoming a grown-up. Consequently, you need to adapt the strategies you use to suit these older children. When working with learners at the top of the primary school:

- **Take them seriously:** at this age, children often see themselves as more grown up than they are. If you want them to behave in a mature way, take their feelings seriously. Never talk down to them. Treat them as the young adults they will soon be, and they may well surprise you by living up to your expectations.

- **Offer a positive role model:** positive role models become particularly important at this age, as children start to understand that their parents are not the whole world. They start paying more attention to external influences, including their peer group and their teachers. You might invite a secondary school learner in to offer them a positive example and to talk to them about what the move to the 'big school' entails.

- **Know what interests them:** at this age children start to take a keen interest in the wider world, and the cultural icons surrounding them in the media. They are starting to gain their independence, and their parents may be giving them more freedom to choose their own clothes and music, or to stay out later in the evenings. Stay up to date with trends (the latest Netflix show, the popular footballers) and find out what interests your class. Incorporate some of this into your teaching or, at the very least, show that you have some knowledge about it.

- **Understand their fears and concerns:** at this age children become very sensitive to peer-group pressure. They may be fearful of being left out of the group, so could succumb to negative pressures to behave inappropriately. They may start to feel embarrassed about relationships with the opposite gender – be sensitive about the kind of groups you ask them to work in.

Handling the transition

The transition to secondary school can be a very difficult time for learners. They are full of concerns about what secondary school will be like. Moving from one teacher to many is also a huge change for them. Do what you can to minimise any negative effects of the transition on both behaviour and learning. Some schools now have a member of staff who has the responsibility for helping children to make a smooth transition. To ease their path, you could:

- **Organise visits:** bring secondary learners into your classroom, or arrange a visit so that your Year 6 children can go to their new secondary school. Similarly, if children come into your Reception class from local pre-schools, do a two-way visit to help prepare them for primary school.

- **Talk through the differences:** talk with your children about the differences between primary and secondary school. Give them advice on coping with having different teachers for different subjects, and on moving around the school rather than staying in one classroom.

- **Help them to get organised:** talk to your children about how they might best organise themselves – they can get the hang of this over the summer before they start at secondary school. For example, ensuring that they have the right equipment, packing their bags the night before school, getting their uniform out and ready to put on in the morning.

- **Pen pals:** get your Year 6 learners to make pen pals with some Year 7 counterparts in local schools. By exchanging letters or emails, they can find out the 'truth' about secondary school. Hopefully this will help dispel many of those rumours that amazingly still float around, such as having your head flushed down the toilet. Having a 'contact' at secondary school can also lessen the fear when they start at the new school. They will know at least one person when they arrive.

- **Mentors:** some schools now offer older mentors to pair up with primary learners in their first year of secondary school. These mentors typically come from Years 9 or 10. Again, it is useful for young learners to have a contact to help them settle in.

- **Shared topics:** some schools now link up to do a shared topic in the final term of primary, which then moves with the child into the first year at secondary. The Year 6 and Year 7 teachers work together to find a topic that will inspire their learners.

Chapter 12
Managing Behaviour: Secondary and Further Education (11+)

Behaviour with young people and adults

Although all the techniques described in this book will help you to manage behaviour more effectively, there are certain approaches that work particularly well with older learners. Often, it's a case of adapting the basic technique to suit the age and type of the learners you have. Those teachers working in a secondary school or sixth-form college or further education college have to deal with learners of all different ages. During the day, you might see pre-teens, teenagers, young adults and adult learners (sometimes even within the same class). Learning to adapt your style to fit each of these age groups is an important teaching technique for you, requiring great subtlety and skill.

Working with older learners is very rewarding – you get to teach your subject at a level that stretches and challenges both you and them. However, it can also be one of the most challenging teaching situations when behaviour is a problem. Some of your learners might be physically larger than you: if they become confrontational, you may feel threatened and vulnerable. By this age, disaffection with education can cause problems with motivation. Some learners at further education level will have had a particularly bad experience of school, and may project this on to you and your lessons.

At the top end of the age range, you'll be working with learners who are adults, or who are almost grown up. They will have many adult concerns that are nothing to do with education. These concerns can sometimes get in the way of their learning, and some may need additional support from you and your setting, beyond what happens in class. With this age range there's also all the pressure of taking and passing exams, and getting ready to move into the full-time work environment.

Starting out

The first few lessons with any class are vital in setting the scene for a successful year. For teachers working in secondary schools and colleges, the beginning of term means meeting and getting to know large numbers of learners. Learning names is a real issue, especially for the teacher of a 'once-a-week' subject, who may be teaching hundreds of different learners each week. Below I look at how you need to establish and communicate your style, set your key standards, and get patterns in place, during those first few weeks.

A question of style

With this age range, your personal teaching style becomes particularly important in getting appropriate behaviour. What you have to decide (ahead of time) is what approach will work best with each of your classes. You need to take into account the kind of organisation you're working within. If this is a tough place to work, with lots of disaffected learners, you're going to have to take a slightly different tack to the one you would take in a less challenging environment.

In a secondary school...

Your learners are moving from class to class, and encountering lots of different kinds of teachers. They will be making decisions about how to behave, based on their judgements about the effectiveness of your style. Your reputation around the school will also impact on their views of you, and of how they should behave for you. Your style plays a critical part in creating a reputation for effectiveness.

In a college...

Your learners are (mostly) there out of some measure of choice – many of them are no longer in the statutory part of their education. They will be seeing themselves as 'adult learners' for the first time, capable of making decisions about whether they are being taught well or not. Some younger college learners choosing a vocational pathway will have done so because they didn't get on with the academic side of school.

What kind of style should I use?

In my opinion, what you're after is to be 'as tough as you feel you can get away with' – the 'no-nonsense' style if you like. You need to get the learners to view you as:

- firm
- confident
- here to make learning happen.

This doesn't mean that you 'shouldn't smile until Christmas', as the old adage goes. What I've found, though, is that learners actually prefer, and respect, a teacher who works in a firm and no-nonsense way from the start. There is no room for messing about; the learning takes absolute priority. Being no-nonsense does not mean:

- being rude
- being negative
- reacting aggressively
- getting into confrontations.

Being no-nonsense does mean:

- being certain and definite about your standards
- being clear about how your lessons will run
- staying calm no matter what the provocation
- knowing when to bend rather than break.

Generally speaking, with the youngest secondary school learners, you can play it fairly firm: 'I'm the teacher and this is exactly what you will do in my lessons'. By the time you get to 15-year-olds and above, you need to temper the toughness with a bit of laid-back cool. Take into account their 'nearly adult' status, so it's more: 'Don't mess with me guys, you'll regret it'. If you're working with adults, you'll need to use a workplace-type approach, where a manager might effectively say to them: 'Here's the line; don't step over it'.

Let's take one example – getting your learners into your room – and look at the way you could communicate a 'no-nonsense' style with different age groups.

For example...

11–13 years

You're standing in the doorway when the learners arrive. You get them to line up outside the classroom, single file, facing front, in silence, before they're allowed inside. As they enter, you check for any uniform infringements, giving positive comments to those whose uniform is perfect. You get anyone who isn't in proper uniform to step to one side and sort it out, before being allowed in.

14–16 years

You're standing in the doorway, leaning against the doorpost to suggest how relaxed you are. You let the learners in as they arrive, welcoming them to your lesson and dealing with any really obvious issues, such as trainers rather than shoes (in a school) or a learner chatting on their phone (in a college).

17+ years

You're sitting on your desk when the learners arrive. You welcome them in, glancing at your watch to indicate that you're ready to get started. Once about half the class is in the room, you stand up and move towards the door and poke your head out. You use a hand signal to show the rest of the learners that they need to get a move on. You begin to pull the door shut, to indicate, 'we're starting now'.

In some very challenging teaching situations, you'll need to tread carefully with a no-nonsense style. Make sure you come over as assertive rather than aggressive. Similarly, with some particularly difficult learners, you're going to need to take a more laid-back, relaxed approach, coaxing them into doing what you want, rather than it being a demand. Do this where you know the only alternative would be a confrontational learner: 'whatever works' is a good rule of thumb.

Don't feel bad about being the one in charge – someone has to be, you're the one being paid to be in charge, and most of your learners want it to be you anyway. Because if it's not you, then it'll be one or more of them, and the most difficult ones will tend to take over and run the place. Once that happens, those who do want to learn something can't, and that's the worst of all possible worlds.

Once you've got the learners behaving and learning as you wish, you can gradually relax your style. This provides you with a useful carrot – 'If I see you all working really sensibly, I'll let you talk quietly while you write.' Don't relax too soon or too suddenly, particularly in your first year of teaching. The first half-term is about the right length of time for you to communicate your no-nonsense style and to cement your reputation as a teacher 'not to be messed with'.

Setting the standards

Before you meet your classes, you've got to decide for yourself which expectations or standards are completely non-negotiable: which things you are willing to 'fight to the death' for. I have certain key standards that I will *never* let drop: no matter if I'm teaching young children, teenagers or adults; no matter if the learners are easy or the most difficult ones I've ever met. The day I let these expectations of behaviour drop would be the day that I would think very seriously about not working in education any more.

However, that is not to say that these things are easy to achieve, or that I always manage to get them right. In some teaching situations they will be nigh on impossible – they will take every ounce of your energy, and then some. But you've got to keep your aims in mind, and strive constantly to achieve them, because otherwise you've effectively told your learners '*whatever*'. Your standards need to be:

- realistic and achievable; but also
- high enough to let learning happen.

My key standards would be:

- We have *one voice.*
- We *respect* each other.
- We always *give it our best.*

Remember, the way you phrase these standards will vary according to the age of the learners. Here's an example of how I might phrase my first standard for different age groups. (You may well wish to phrase yours differently – whatever works for you.)

For example...

11–13 years

'My expectation is of 'one voice', so I expect everyone to listen in complete silence when someone is addressing the whole group, whether that's me or one of you. And I want to see focused attention while you're listening.'

14–16 years

'I really need you to listen to me, and to each other, so we can get on with learning. Does anyone have any questions about that? Because 'one voice' is an absolute in my classroom.'

17+ years

'The most important thing for me is that there is one voice. That we listen properly to each other, and when I need to talk to you, you listen properly to me too. And we're going to listen to each other in silence – anyone have any thoughts about why that's important?'

When you're setting your standards, particularly at the lower-secondary age range, it's often the small things that count. If you let your learners get away with something small, this sends a signal that other things are up for negotiation. To push on the small things, you might:

- Insist that written work is done in silence, so they can concentrate. Offset this with the 'generous gift' of two-minute time-outs to talk.
- Adhere like glue to uniform rules, such as coats off, no trainers, ties done up properly.
- Stamp down on small breaches of the rules, for instance, the chewing of gum.

The older the learners, the more you might decide to 'overlook' very small infringements of the rules. If a disaffected 16-year-old has their tie slightly undone, but is working, you're not going to want to bother them. But you can also quietly make it clear that you're 'overlooking' this rule-breaking because they are getting on with their work.

Setting up the patterns

As well as setting your standards, at the start of the year you should also set up the pattern of how your lessons will run. These patterns are vital where learners are being taught by a number of different teachers. They need to see a well-structured, clear and consistent pattern to your lessons, so they feel secure about how to behave for you.

You can see an example of a teacher setting up a lesson pattern in Chapter 2 ('Establishing the pattern of your lessons/days', page 26). When thinking about the pattern you want, consider the following questions:

- What do I want my learners to do when they first arrive at my lesson?
- Where am I when they arrive at the room?
- How do they know where to sit? Is this a free choice or not?
- At what point, and how, are resources and equipment put on desks?
- What do I do about taking a register, and how do the learners behave while I do that?
- How do I explain the learning that's going to take place in the lesson?
- How should the learners behave while I'm explaining the lesson?
- What kind of working atmosphere do I want?
- How do we deal with resources and equipment?
- What happens to finish off the lesson?
- How do learners behave while getting ready to leave the room?
- How do I dismiss the class?

Your pattern will depend on how 'formal' you want or need your lessons to be. If you're working with the youngest learners in a very traditional classroom environment, you're probably going to go for a highly structured approach. If you're working with adult vocational learners in a workshop-type setting, you're not going to want or need such a tightly controlled style.

Seven key strategies for success

Below I explain seven key strategies and approaches that are particularly useful in a secondary school or further education setting.

1 Be inventive to get their attention

When you need to talk to the whole class, you've got to have their attention. If you don't, consider the signals you're sending: basically, you're saying you don't mind them not listening to you, that you don't believe you have enough control to get them to listen, and that what you're saying really isn't all that important.

With some (perhaps many) classes in this age range, this can be a difficult aim to achieve. I too have stood at the front of a class, waiting for their attention and feeling certain that I will never fulfil my aim. I am fully aware of how nerve-racking it feels, and how tempting it is to give in and just start talking anyway, even though some learners aren't listening.

There are many different ways you can get your learners to pay attention, and the best strategies are the inventive, imaginative and interesting ones. Have a look at the following ideas and see which ones might work for you, or how you can adapt them to use with your classes.

- **Written note to the class:** look sad, move to your board, and write or type: 'If you won't all be silent and let me get on with teaching you, then unfortunately I'm going to have to turn to consequences, and I really don't want to have to do that.' By the time you're halfway through writing this, hopefully the class will be looking to see what you're doing.

- **The theatrical gesture:** try this if you have a bit of the drama queen in your soul. At the very least, you'll get your learners' attention and raise a laugh. Pretend to bang your head on your desk and start sobbing, saying, 'Why, oh why won't they be silent? I just can't cope any more. Oh, what am I going to do?!'

- **Speak my language:** ask the class for a suitable call and response that you could use to get their attention. The teacher who originally gave me this idea told me that her inner-city teenagers went for the following. Teacher: *'Oyyy!'* Learners: *'You wot?'*

2 Treat them as adults

Learners live up (or down) to what you expect of them. Treat them like adults and you may be surprised at the mature way in which they respond. Some will let you down, but you should not let the behaviour of a minority prevent you from doing something with the attentive, hard-working majority. The older the learners are, the more adult the way in which you can treat them.

In return for you treating them as adults, they have a responsibility to behave and work appropriately. Make it clear to your learners that this is a partnership: if they don't fulfil their end of the bargain, you are entitled to withdraw any privileges you've given.

To treat them as adults, you should:

- give them your trust
- give them a chance to prove themselves to you, rather than assuming the worst
- let them get hands on with equipment and resources, even if you're not sure how they will respond
- speak to them as you would to a fellow worker, as if you worked in an office.

And make sure you don't:

- patronise them (temper your use of tone with older learners)
- speak down to them

- suggest (by your body language, vocabulary, actions) that they are somehow 'below' you, just because they are younger.

3 But sometimes... treat them as children

Paradoxically, older learners also respond well to the teacher who uses childlike approaches from time to time. Education at this stage can be very serious and highly pressured; it's important to let them blow off steam on occasions. You could:

- play some games with them
- do a fun, light-hearted quiz
- set up a really messy activity
- find an excuse to do some dressing up
- hand out some childlike rewards – stickers, lollies, bubbles.

And when you give them the go-ahead to act like children, it'll work even better if you join in the activity too.

4 Blame the policy

The older the learners, the more they tend to 'fight back' when a teacher gives them a consequence. When this happens, it can mean that:

- the teacher and learner get into an argument
- the learner backs themselves into a corner and gets thrown out
- the teacher avoids disciplining because they want to avoid confrontation.

Clearly, there will be times when it is necessary to use a consequence: what you need to do is find a way to do this without getting into confrontations. To achieve this, use the technique of 'blame the policy'. Remember that your main role here is not to discipline – you are here to teach. The only reason you discipline is to allow you to *get on with the teaching*. When you blame the policy, this demonstrates to the learner that the behaviour is *between them and the institution*, rather than *between you and them*.

In order to be in a position to blame the policy, you need to know what the policy is in the first place. Be one hundred per cent certain: know the rules on chewing gum, mobile phones, jewellery, coats, trainers, swearing, and so on. Otherwise, you'll find that when your learners challenge you about the consequence, you come across as unsure and you're tempted to back down. Have a paper copy of the school behaviour policy or the college disciplinary procedures to hand at all times.

Here's a (slightly tongue-in-cheek) example of a teacher 'blaming the policy', with a college-aged learner, to show you what I mean.

For example...

The teacher has asked Harry three times to get on with some work. He currently has his feet up on the table and is staring out of the window.

Teacher: Harry, I notice that you have ignored my previous three requests to get on with some work.

Harry: What you gonna do 'bout it?

Teacher: [*whipping out his copy of the college disciplinary procedures*] Well Harry, I think you'll find [*leafs through pages*] that under Clause 3, sub-section (ii) of the disciplinary policy, it says that 'Learners who repeatedly refuse to comply with a reasonable request should be asked to leave the lesson'.

Harry: [*completely confused by this*] Huh?!?

Teacher: Harry, you have a choice. Feet down, get on with the work. Refuse to comply, leave the lesson. Up to you.

---

5 Make the learning real

In Chapter 7, I looked at how you can teach for positive behaviours. In the secondary school and in further education, one of the key features in that aspiration is to make the learning real. This is particularly important for learners who are engaged in a vocational or work-based course at college. They simply have to see the links between what they are learning and the job that they could get once they qualify.

In the secondary school, those really disruptive teenagers who cause you so much misery often turn into totally different people when they go on a work-experience placement. They begin to see how the adult world of work is out there waiting for them, just around the corner. The reward of a salary, and the freedom that having money can bring, is a fantastic 'carrot' for learners of this age. Equally, though, they have to accept that inappropriate behaviour in the workplace has a definitive outcome – the potential to lose your job.

When you 'make the learning real', you clarify and underline this link between what happens in school or college, and what happens in the adult world beyond. To 'make it real', you could:

- Set up workplace-style scenarios: for instance, a 'scene' from a building site, with various hazards to identify. Get the learners to work 'in character' as health and safety inspectors, to find as many hazards as they can.

- Include plenty of resources: make the resources you use as real, and as 'hands on', as possible. If there's an option to go for a real or a toy version of an item, choose the real item in preference.

- Demonstrate the importance of theory: learners in this age range love being taught technical-sounding terms – my Year 7 learners have loved the idea of learning about 'pathetic fallacy' in their English classes. Show how this theory links to the reality of the subject, and make 'doing the theory' a condition for 'doing the practical bits'.

- Get out of the classroom: some of my very best experiences as a teacher have been outside the classroom walls. You could try taking a GCSE class to the theatre, or a group of young children to a farm. By taking your class into the real world, you show them that education and learning are everywhere.

6 Show your human side

When you're working with older learners, the approaches you use can generally be a bit closer to the edge than those you might use with young children. How far you go depends both on your personal philosophies of education, and on what your setting finds acceptable.

Although you want to enforce consistent boundaries, you also need to take into account that sometimes in life we want to push at and stretch the boundaries – to rebel a little against what 'authority' says we must do.

For instance, you know that your Year 9 learners would respond well to being bribed with some chocolate, but your school's healthy eating policy means you're not meant to have sweets in school. What do you do? Or, your most difficult learner only ever does any work if you 'overlook' the fact that he is wearing his headphones. Again, what's the best thing to do? (There's no right or wrong answer; you have to make the professional judgement for yourself.)

You can also show that you're human by:

- laughing at yourself when you make a mistake
- sharing some of your interests with learners (which football team you support, that kind of thing)
- giving them, as well as yourself, the occasional relaxed lesson
- sharing a few fun anecdotes from your life outside of education.

Come across as someone who is self-deprecating, particularly with older learners where you don't need to maintain your 'teacher' image quite so much.

7 Be an inspiration

When you set out to work in education, I'm sure you didn't do so because you 'just needed a job'. Being in the profession is too tough to do it just for a living wage: the vast majority of people do it because they care about making a difference. Working with learners of 11 years and above, you are (hopefully) teaching them the subject that you love. Never lose sight of how lucky you are to be working all day with the subject that inspires you. Aim to pass your inspiration and your love of the subject on to your learners.

When learners sense that their teacher *really cares* about their subject, they cannot help but be at least a little bit interested too. Remember, some of those learners sitting in front of you will one day choose to study this subject in depth, perhaps to degree level or even beyond. Maybe they will even come to teach it too, at some point in the future. If you can be at least partly responsible for that decision, what a wonderful thing to achieve. To be an inspiration, you'll need to:

- put energy and enthusiasm into your teaching
- get creative with your approaches, and take some risks
- use your face, voice and body in an imaginative way
- choose a teaching style that engages or interests
- model an attitude to learning that your learners can learn from
- model the kind of behaviour you want your learners to emulate.

The form tutor and behaviour

Those of you working as secondary teachers or college tutors will often be expected to take on a pastoral role within your setting. As a tutor, you register your group and take responsibility for their overall progress and welfare. Working with a form group is a very different prospect to working with a class in a subject area. In fact, you might not be timetabled to teach any of your form-group learners at all.

How you handle behaviour with your form group depends on two main factors: the expectations of the school or college as to how form tutors should work, and the age and type of learners in the group. On the whole, you can afford to take a more relaxed approach to the role of form tutor than class teacher. Adapt the style you use as a subject teacher, and develop a different kind of relationship with these learners. This more relaxed relationship is important, because your form tutees may be coming to you with personal or social concerns, and they need to feel free to talk openly.

Match your approaches to the age group

If you are given a group in their first year at secondary school, you have a wonderful chance to 'train them up' in your ways of working. Start out with a fairly firm approach, then relax a little over time. If you're given a rowdy group in their last year of schooling, who have had four different tutors over the years, there is little point giving yourself a stressful time by trying to lay down the law too hard.

Keep a check on equipment

With younger learners, help them to organise themselves properly, and to avoid pointless consequences for missing equipment, etc. With a group who are new to secondary, you might do an equipment check at the start of each day/week.

Keep an overview of consequences and rewards

Many schools use diaries for learners, where teachers can record consequences and rewards earned. Take an overview of how well (or badly) each learner is doing by looking at their diaries. If necessary, provide an early alert system for a more senior staff member, such as a head of year or house.

Sort out the issues that waste lesson time

Act as a useful support and backup for subject teachers, by sorting out those minor issues that eat into lesson time. Ensure that your learners have shoes on rather than trainers, and uniform sorted, before they head off for the day's lessons.

Consider how best to take the register

With younger tutees, you will probably be able to insist on and get total silence to complete the register. With some older classes, such an approach will only set you up for confrontations. If you are likely to have difficulty getting the class to be silent, ask for a volunteer to help you check who is and is not present. Take the register yourself, though – it's a legal document and your responsibility.

Keep a teacher/tutor divide

If you teach members of your form group, you need to make it clear to them that the two roles are distinct. Have a quiet word with any individuals who push at the boundaries, clarifying the different roles that you play in class and in tutor time.

Chapter 13
Common Behaviour Issues

Ten strategies for dealing with common behaviour issues

It is typically the case that it is constant low-level disruption that is hardest for teachers to deal with. These are the problems that are not so serious that they require a high-level intervention, but that are wearing for the teacher, and that cut into the learning time available. In this chapter, I look at some of the most common behaviour issues you might face in your classroom, and offer you ten strategies that should help you deal with each one.

1 Straying off task

The teacher sets the task clearly, but after a short time at work, some of the learners become distracted and lose their focus. To help you solve this issue:

- Set a short time limit and use a visual indicator to show time passing, e.g. an egg timer.
- Set a clear target for how much work must be done in this time.
- Pull the class back together when the time is up to get feedback on progress.
- Go and sit with those learners you know struggle most to stay on task.
- Ask your teaching assistant to support these learners in keeping their focus.
- Consider the nature of the activities you set and differentiate or scaffold so that all learners can access them.
- Identify those learners who are staying on task, and praise them verbally, specifically and loudly enough for the whole class to hear.
- Agree a visual warning system for 'on-task behaviour' with several levels, for instance, a set of cards.

- When a learner strays off task, give them a card so they have a visual reminder of the warning.
- Give the learner a choice – do the activity now, or do it in break time.

2 Lack of listening skills

Some learners really struggle to listen and process what you are saying, when you are addressing the whole class. Even if they are silent, they do not appear to take in the information you give them. To help you address this issue:

- If a learner is not listening, pause in your explanation. Wait without saying anything until the learner looks towards you to see why you have paused. Smile and say 'thank you for your attention', then continue with your explanation.
- Get those learners who struggle to listen to sit closest to the front, so you can keep an eye on them.
- Lower the volume of your voice, to encourage close listening.
- Back up your verbal explanations with visual ones too – for instance, writing ideas up on the board.
- Ask the learners to help you 'be teacher', by taking part in the explanation or writing up the ideas for you.
- Build up the length of listening time gradually – keep a check on how much teacher talk you use at any one time.
- Let the learners 'do' something when you are talking, for instance, writing their ideas on a mini whiteboard.
- Get the learners physically involved when you are talking – something as simple as thumbs up/down if they agree/disagree can work well, or the use of mini whiteboards to share ideas.

3 Shouting 'I've finished!'

Some of the learners rush through the tasks you set, without taking care over their work. They then shout out 'I've finished!' and expect an immediate response from an adult. To help you overcome this problem:

- Have an expectation of 'three before me', where you ask that the learners take three steps to improve their work, before they say it is 'finished'. This might be: check it again, look up any spellings you're unsure about in a dictionary, ask a friend to read it through and comment.

- Be clear about what the extension task is for anyone who finishes the activity early – set this up during your initial explanation.

- For written tasks, you can set a target for how many words will be written, or how many paragraphs completed, before the piece can be considered 'finished'.

- Have a clear rule about not shouting out in class, and a consistent consequence for those who continue to do it.

- Move around the class, noting who is working quickly, and giving them feedback on what they should do next.

- Spend some lesson time looking at the skills of planning, drafting and re-drafting, and why these are important.

- Encourage the learners to focus on improving their work by taking a 'finished' piece and re-drafting it.

- Have a specific target for the activity, personalised to each learner as far as possible, for instance, 'to put all your full stops in the right places'.

- If a learner has genuinely finished, you could ask them to support someone else in completing the activity.

- Consider why the learners are rushing to 'be first to finish' – have you subconsciously made 'finishing' seem like the main goal?

4 Shouting 'This is easy!'

Some of the more confident learners are in the habit of commenting on the work as they do it, shouting out how 'easy' it is. Their assessment of the difficulty of the activity does not necessarily match with their ability to complete it properly. To address this issue:

- Consider whether the activity might actually be too easy for some of the learners – look for ways to offer additional challenge.

- Have a clear rule about shouting out in class, and clarify the consequences of doing this.

- Ask the learners whether they can think of any ways of making the activity harder.

- Encourage your learners to play a part in creating activities, for instance, by making a list of questions that they would like to answer during a topic.

- Ask the learners to swap their work with someone else, to see how well their peers have managed to complete the activity.

- Have a choice of several activities, so that learners can pick one that matches their interests and attainment levels.

- You could grade activities 'red' for difficult, 'orange' for medium and 'green' for easy.

- You can then ask learners to choose at least one (or more) activity from each category, to complete during the lesson.

- Give the learners a set of criteria for marking their work, and ask them to perform a self-assessment.

- Get the learners to grade themselves according to how 'well' they think they did; then see whether this grading matches up with yours when you mark the work.

5 Shouting out the answers

Some of the learners regularly shout out their answers during whole-class question and answer sessions. They don't seem to realise that being 'super keen' is not helpful for everyone's learning. To deal with this issue:

- When a learner shouts out, pointedly ignore that learner – just don't 'hear' or respond to them.

- Focus your attention on those who have their hands up, praising them instead.

- Always get your answer from a learner who has waited to be asked, even if the answer is the same as the one that was shouted out.

- Consider whether asking for 'hands up' is part of the problem – try using other strategies for whole-class question and answer sessions as well.

- When you ask a question, get the learners to discuss their thoughts in pairs before you ask for the answer.

- If one learner regularly shouts out, try getting that learner to come up to the front and 'be teacher', asking some of the questions for you.

- Give each learner a mini whiteboard and ask them to write their answers down, to show you simultaneously.

- Talk with individuals who always shout out, to help them understand why it is important for you to hear from other learners as well.

- Suggest a strategy that learners could use to stop themselves from being tempted to shout out, to encourage self-control and self-discipline. For instance, they might put a hand over their mouths every time you ask a question.

6 A flat refusal to join in with the lesson

Some of your learners point blank refuse to join in with your lessons, or to complete their work. To handle this issue:

- Have a clear expectation that 'we all join in' and 'we all try our hardest in lessons'.

- Explain why this is important, talking about group cooperation and the best use of lesson learning time.

- Clarify the consequences of a refusal to join in, so that all learners know what their choices are.

- Take a consistent response to a refusal to work, applying the same consequence every time.

- Consider whether the learner is refusing to work to cover up an inability to access the learning.

- Give learners every chance to make the right choice, by supporting them at the start of an activity.

- Aim not to back learners into a corner – leave a metaphorical 'door open' so that they have the chance to make the right decision.

- Sometimes it can work to ignore the refusal to learn – learners may come to the learning of their own doing if you give them some time to consider their options.

- Offer some kind of choice, to make the learners feel like they have agency. For instance, saying, 'Do you want to start with this task first, or this one?'

- Look for motivators as well – offer a reward for those who settle straight to task and work as hard as possible.

- Consider whether you can make the learning seem so tempting to do, that the learner is hard put not to want to join in.

7 Swinging on chairs

Some of your learners will repeatedly tip back on their chairs and swing around on them during lessons. You worry that this is both a safety issue, and possibly also a symptom of their distraction from learning. To deal with this problem:

- Have a clear expectation of 'four chair legs on the floor at all times'.

- Use a visual signal as a reminder of your expectation – holding four fingers downwards when you spot a learner tipping back on a chair.

- Talk with your learners about *why* this is important – emphasise the dangers of tipping backwards and make it clear that this rule is for their own safety.

- Have a consistent consequence for those learners who repeatedly refuse to sit properly.

- One potential consequence might be to say to the learners that they will have to stand up for a while, if they choose not to sit properly.

- Consider whether the tipping behaviour is a sign that the learners would benefit from a physical outlet during lessons.

- Incorporate opportunities to get up and move around during lessons, for instance, taking a 'learning walk' to look at other learners' books.

- Create an interesting reward to give to those children who always sit properly – in a primary classroom this could be the chance to sit on a special cushion or chair at carpet time.

- Sometimes it can help to rearrange your classroom layout, to 'jolt' the learners out of their normal habits.

- If suitable for your teaching space and subject, you might clear all the chairs to the sides, and teach your learners while sitting on the floor.

8 'Accidentally' forgetting something/needing to leave class

Some learners repeatedly turn up at lessons without the appropriate materials – book, planner, kit. They then ask to leave the lesson to go and collect their resources. Other learners make requests to go to the toilets far more often than you would like. You're pretty sure that this is just a way to get out of working for some of them. To handle this situation:

- Be very clear about the equipment that children need to bring to your lessons, and whether you will give anyone permission to leave the room during class time – clarify this in your first session together.

- Have a consistent consequence for a failure to bring the right materials.

- To show a bit of flexibility, you could give your learners one 'get out of forgotten materials free' card. They have one chance to forget, and use their card, but after that point they automatically receive the consequence.

- If a number of learners always forget the same resource (e.g. pencils/pens), consider having a stock of this resource available to save disruptions. You could 'hire out' your resources in lieu of a small donation to the charity pot.

- Alternatively, have an amusing 'I forgot my pen' consequence, such as having to use a particularly fluffy and embarrassing spare pen. I once met a teacher who had a *Frozen* pen that played 'Let it Go', which he would offer to learners who had forgotten theirs. Funnily enough, they always seemed to find their own pens instead.

- Stand at the door and ask learners to show that they have their materials/kit before they enter.

- For young children, for any learners who have bowel problems or who suffer from urinary infections, and for teenagers who are menstruating, there may be a genuine need to visit the toilets during lessons. Create a clear structure for how this happens. For instance, the learners could wear a band or have a card, to show that they have your permission to visit the toilet.

9 Saying 'it wasn't me' when you saw the learner do it

Sometimes, when you challenge learners about their behaviour, they claim that 'it wasn't me'. This happens even when you have just seen the behaviour, and you know that it *was* them. You are finding their denials increasingly irritating. To handle this issue:

- Completely fail to hear the 'it wasn't me' comment – pretend you didn't hear it at all.

- Refuse to get dragged into 'Oh yes it was', 'Oh no it wasn't' style arguments.

- Simply restate what you saw, and what the consequence of this behaviour will be.

- Encourage learners to take responsibility, by using the language of choice to help them manage their behaviour.

- Help learners understand that their behaviour is separate to them as a person, by using language that blames the behaviour and not the learner.

- If the learner continues to argue, repeat the choice without getting dragged into a debate.

- Consider doing some lesson activities around rights and responsibilities.

- Talk as a group about why it is important to be honest, and the issues that can arise if we are not.

- Find ways to maintain your calm, because irritation can encourage you to take a less rational approach.

- Make it clear that once a consequence is served, the learner gets to 'start over' in your estimation – that you never hold a grudge.

10 Wanting to be invisible

Some learners seem to want to fade into the background during your lessons. They sit quietly, and are not disruptive, but very rarely contribute anything to discussions. To address this issue:

- Take a gentle, step-by-step approach to building learners' confidence.
- Don't force a learner to speak or get involved if it seems to be causing them anxiety.
- Find ways for learners to contribute non-verbally, for instance, by using visual responses such as a thumbs-up for agreement.
- Give one-to-one input to less confident learners, when the whole class is on task.
- Use supportive language, building self-esteem slowly.
- Praise the learner's efforts if or when they do choose to get involved.
- Create group activities where learners can take a 'quiet' role, for instance, being a resource monitor or a scribe for their group.
- Encourage learners to talk to you about their interests, and consider incorporating these into lessons.
- Help learners gain access to extra curricular activities aimed at boosting confidence. For instance, you might help them to get involved in the backstage team in a school production.

Part Four

When Things Get Tough

Chapter 14
Managing Confrontation

Why do confrontations arise?

There are many reasons why confrontations arise. Sometimes the cause will be entirely outside your control – a learner arrives at your classroom in such a tense and worked-up state that there is little you can do beyond containing the situation. Some learners carry with them a huge weight of metaphorical baggage – traumatic situations and events experienced outside of the school setting that make them far more likely to blow a fuse. Some will have learnt by example, from parents or carers who react to problems in a confrontational manner. Some might have experienced serious child protection issues, which mean that their social, emotional and mental health has been badly affected.

Wherever possible, within the bounds of confidentiality, it is worth your having at least some idea of the kind of home lives that your learners lead. You can then be sensitive to their particular circumstances, applying the flexibility discussed at the start of this book. Remember, it is not the standards that need to be flexible, but the approaches that you take to get to the standards. Just as you would adapt your approaches to support everyone to learn in different subject areas, so you can adapt your approaches to support everyone in learning how to behave.

If we are completely honest with ourselves, there may be times when the teacher probably contributes, at least partly, to the confrontation arising. While it is not the teacher's *fault* when a learner loses control, they do certain things which exacerbate the situation. In your quest to manage behaviour better, it is important to understand how you might contribute to confrontations, so that you can avoid them whenever possible. This is not to blame or criticise you – teaching is a stressful job and inevitably we make mistakes. Instead, this is to encourage you to reflect on the areas in which you can develop your skills.

Here are some ways that the teacher can inadvertently create the climate for a confrontation. (Please note, these are all mistakes I have made myself, over the years.)

The mood of the teacher

When the teacher begins a lesson in a bad mood, this attitude filters through and puts everyone in the room in a negative frame of mind. They might be unnecessarily picky or uncompromising with the learners, and consequently generate an atmosphere of tension.

A sense of unfairness

Learners are very sensitive to actual or perceived unfairness. We would all hope to be completely fair all or most of the time. However, as teachers we need to be conscious that sometimes our personal feelings about individuals can subconsciously come out in the way that we treat them.

Misunderstandings

Sometimes the teacher accuses a learner or class of inappropriate behaviour and is entirely wrong. I once caught some learners passing around what I assumed was a note at the back of the room. When I insisted they hand it over, they refused and I got cross. In the end it turned out that they were all signing a thank-you card for me. Whoops!

Playing to the 'audience'

If you take on a rude learner in front of the class, this sets the stage for a confrontation. While some learners will back down, others will be unable or unwilling to do so, and will get themselves trapped into a slanging match with you.

Lack of consistency

Where the teacher is inconsistent, this can create a sense of injustice and consequently lead to tensions. It might be that the teacher applies the rules differently from other staff in the school. It could be that the teacher varies their expectations from day to day. The more consistent you are, the more your learners will know what to expect from you.

Prejudging the learner or class

Once a learner gets a reputation, it can be hard to shift. Similarly, a class is sometimes known as 'difficult' by a number of staff in a school. When the teacher meets a learner or a class with preset expectations, it means the learners are never given the chance to prove themselves. Again, this can create a sense of injustice and consequently lead to tension and confrontation.

How to avoid confrontation

Wherever possible, it is obviously far preferable to avoid getting into confrontations in the first place: they can only ever do damage to the relationship between you and your learners. In addition, there is always the risk that a negative encounter might spiral out of control into physical aggression.

Problems can occur particularly when the teacher is tired and stressed. A learner swears at you or behaves in a completely inappropriate way, and it is all too easy (and natural) to want to confront the behaviour in a similarly hostile way, thus escalating the situation. Avoiding confrontation does not mean you avoid dealing with the issue, but rather that you approach the problem in a way that is more likely to calm the situation than inflame it. When handling a confrontational learner, use the following techniques:

- **Be an assertive, confident and consistent teacher:** If you manage the class in an effective and assertive way all or most of the time, you should be rewarded with lower levels of tension within the group more generally.

- **Be aware of your emotional state:** On those days when you are tired or tense, have an awareness of how this might affect your classroom management skills. Minimise potential stress by keeping lesson activities simple and controlled. Make sure you take your breaks and leave school on time to get a good rest.

- **Keep difficult interactions private:** Learn to talk with and discipline learners in a private way, so that there is no risk of them playing up to an audience of their peers.

- **Make an early intervention:** Keep an eye out for the early signs of any problems. If you notice an argument starting, or a learner becoming restless, intervene straight away, for instance, by using a distraction.

- **Know when to ignore low-level inappropriate behaviour:** On the other hand, know when it is appropriate to simply ignore silliness, rather than making an issue out of attention-seeking behaviour. Finding this balance is one of the trickiest aspects of handling behaviour.

- **Refuse to enter into tit-for-tat arguments:** Some learners love to drag the teacher into an argument: it means they don't have to work; they might even be able to deflect the blame for inappropriate behaviour. Don't get pulled in – it is pointless and can lead to unnecessary tension. Remember – 'be reasonable but don't reason with them'.

- **Change the subject:** Try using a distraction to dissipate a potential confrontation. Just as, when a baby is crying, you might pull a silly face or shake a favourite toy, so by changing the subject with your learners, you could throw them 'off the track' away from their aggression.

- **Defer the issue:** There will be occasions when you are involved in an interaction and it becomes clear that the learner is simply not going to do as you ask, and instead is getting increasingly agitated. In these cases, it can help to defer the whole discussion until a later time, for instance, saying 'we'll discuss this at the end of class'.

- **Be willing to apologise when you get it wrong:** When you do make a mistake, for instance, if you're rude or unnecessarily aggressive with a learner or the class, have the humility to apologise. This will earn you a great deal of respect.

How to deal with confrontation

Once a confrontation gets started, some learners find it incredibly difficult to back down. As the adult, and the professional, it is your responsibility to try to deal with the situation in the best way possible. The ideal is for you to manage the situation so that the least damage is done to the relationship between you and your learners, while at the same time ensuring the safety of everyone in your class. The following suggestions should help you achieve this.

Behaviour management techniques

'Remove' the problem

Often, a confrontation is about a 'thing', whether this is a toy, a pencil case, a mobile phone, and so on. If possible, get the 'thing' out of the equation. Take care with directly taking the item as your first approach, unless this is a policy in your school – taking something personal from a child can escalate tensions, because of that sense of belonging that we give to our personal items. Instead, you could insist that the learner puts it away in a bag before you are forced to take it away, or that they place it on the table for you to look after. Sometimes you might 'remove' the learner, asking them to step outside the room for a moment, to calm themselves down. Make sure the learner is not left alone: ask a teaching assistant to go with the learner or leave the door open so that you can keep a close eye on them.

Take feelings and complaints seriously

Sometimes it is enough simply to listen. Ask the learner to describe the problem that has led to the blow-up and make the right sympathetic noises. Ask an open question, such as 'What's going on here?' or 'Do you want to tell me what the problem is?'

Know when to send for help: there is no shame at all in sending a reliable learner to get a senior leader if a fight breaks out in your room, or if a situation escalates beyond where you feel comfortable. This will help you to handle the situation, and will also provide you with an adult witness to what takes place.

Remain calm

It's very difficult for a learner to sustain feelings of anger if there is nothing to feed off. Stay calm and it's hard for your learners to maintain a confrontational manner. It also demonstrates a powerful positive role model of how to handle aggression.

Use co-regulation techniques

It can be really helpful to use co-regulation techniques, particularly with younger learners. Name the emotion that you can see, 'I can tell that you're feeling angry because you're clenching your fists.' Encourage them to join in with some self-calming techniques, such as breathing deeply together or transferring the feeling of anger into something inanimate, for instance, pummeling a cushion. Essentially you are narrating the learner's feelings while at the same time offering a model of how to manage angry emotions.

Pause for a moment

When a situation erupts, the temptation is to jump straight in to sort it out. Take a few seconds to think first – giving yourself time to calm down can help you handle a tricky situation in the best possible way.

The teacher's use of voice/body

Use a hypnotic tone of voice

Your voice can be very helpful in calming down a tense situation. Use a slow monotone to dampen down heightened emotions, flattening a normally lively tone.

Use your body language

Similarly, non-confrontational postures and body language can help to calm things down. Make sure you keep out of the learner's personal space – not only to lessen the tension, but also to protect yourself if they end up lashing out.

Make repeated use of names

Repeating a learner's name will help you to get their attention and might even allow you to pull them back from the confrontation. Combine this with a low-key and hypnotic tone of voice.

Remember, it's not about win or lose

Teachers can get trapped into feeling that they have to 'win' a confrontation. The reality is that nobody really wins, no matter what happens in the end. Your aim should be to calm things down, not to end up feeling that you have won.

Remember, you don't have to make eye contact

We are so used to having eye contact with our learners and our classes that it is tempting to get locked into a 'look at me when I'm talking to you' attitude. Sometimes, a better approach is to talk to the learner without looking them directly in the eye.

Handling the aftermath

When a confrontation takes place in one of your lessons, you may find yourself feeling shaky and upset. You might also suffer a dip in self-confidence and feel that you have somehow 'failed' as a teacher. Senior leaders should understand that serious confrontations can have a severe impact on staff, and there should be support available to help you manage the fallout. The following suggestions should hopefully help you to cope and to bounce back quickly.

- Give yourself some time to recover – if possible, ask for your next lesson to be covered so that you get a chance to process what happened.

- Record what took place – get hold of an incident form and write about the confrontation while the details are fresh in your mind. Note the names of witnesses where appropriate.

- Find support wherever it is available – whether this is from leaders, a union, other teachers, or perhaps from an organisation or person outside of the school environment.

- Try not to take the situation personally – a learner who is often verbally or physically abusive obviously has some serious problems that have happened in their past. Even if you feel like you might have somehow triggered the situation, learn to forgive yourself – someone else's aggression is never, in any way, your fault.

- Try not to bear grudges – aim to give the learner a 'fresh start' the next time you have to teach them.

Teaching in the toughest settings

Some of the people reading this book will be teaching in really difficult settings. Many teachers have reported an increase in difficult behaviour since the lockdowns at the start of the pandemic, and you might also be facing issues arising from this. Although any teaching job is going to be a challenge, some settings are at the far end of the scale of 'toughness'. Typically, in the 'toughest' settings:

- The overall ethos of the setting has become negative and hopeless.
- The learners don't feel that their teachers or the leadership team can control them.
- There is a high turnover of staff.
- Because staff leave so quickly, there is no time to build up relationships.
- Learners feel that staff 'don't care' because they keep leaving.
- They are more likely to 'act up' for new teachers to test them out and see whether they can cope.
- The learners start to 'believe their own publicity', and begin to feel that they have to live up to their reputation.
- The setting has a bad reputation locally, and this leads to a fall in learner numbers. Only those who 'have to' go there do.
- There are larger than usual numbers of learners with learning difficulties or severe behavioural issues.

Some teachers work in a 'tough' environment for many years: they stick it out and become part of the backbone of the setting. Others understandably find the pressure too hard to handle, or simply do not want to work in this kind of setting.

If you're working in a really tough setting

Put yourself first

Practise the art of 'selfish altruism'. The idea is that, by being selfish and looking after yourself as a priority, you put yourself in a much better position to help your learners. It also means that you are more likely to survive in a tough setting in the long run. This means you must take your breaks – be firm with yourself about spending time away from the learners. Give yourself permission to teach a less-than-perfect lesson when you're not on top form, without feeling guilty about it.

Work out your priorities

Set yourself some simple, key priorities and stick to these. Work out what you can realistically ask for and get in terms of behaviour, without pulling yourself into endless confrontations. Focus on getting learning to happen, rather than on getting everything exactly as you wish before you start the lesson. That is not to say that you should lower your standards; rather, that you must work out what your key expectations are, and stick to them as far as humanly possible.

Understand learner reputations

In a tough school, the young people quickly learn how important it is to build themselves a 'reputation'. Those who are strongest, who have the quickest wits, or who are willing to challenge authority, gain a status that puts them near the top of the peer-group heap. Behaviour issues in your classroom might often involve a learner trying to assert their reputation. If you can get these 'high status' individuals on your side, you have much more chance of winning over the rest of the group.

Don't pass the buck

In a tough school, metaphorical 'fires' are breaking out all the time, and all over the place. What I mean is, there will be incidents going on in each classroom, and probably in the corridors as well. In a tough school, you have to deal with your own situations where humanly possible, rather than calling for a more senior teacher. This increases your reputation for effectiveness, and allows senior staff to focus on keeping overall control.

Learn to forgive yourself

The more stressful the situation, the more we tend to make mistakes. Whether this is through reacting with a 'fight or flight' response or saying things we later come to regret, if you work in a really tough school you will need to learn to forgive yourself for errors. Of course, this is not to say that you have free rein to say whatever you like to the learners, or to be unprofessional, but do forgive yourself if from time to time you make a mistake. Don't be afraid to own up to it either – usually 'tough' learners will respect you more for being honest when you've done something wrong.

Chapter 15
Managing Stress

I can't cope anymore!

There's no doubt that teaching is a difficult profession in which to work. It is emotionally, physically and psychologically taxing, and there may be times when you do feel as though you just can't cope anymore. No matter how hard you try, it seems you are making no headway in improving the behaviour of your learners. This is extremely demoralising. Day after day, you arrive at your job, only to face learners who simply will not behave. You begin to dread coming into work, knowing that you have to face such difficult days.

At these times, it is important to differentiate between the inevitable ups and downs of a teaching career, and the signs of a more serious problem. Once you've identified exactly what the problem is, you can explore some suitable options for dealing with it.

What's the problem?

The feeling that you can't cope anymore can build up slowly, or it can arrive without warning one day, when you feel that you simply can't get out of bed and go into work. Sometimes, the problem is a temporary one, and one that can be dealt with relatively easily. On the other hand, it could be a long-term issue, and one that will require more extreme measures to solve. Here are some thoughts about what the problem might be.

Seasonal effects

The time of the year can have a huge impact on your ability to cope with difficult behaviour. In September you will be fresh and full of energy, ready to deal with whatever the learners can throw at you. Of course, this is the time when you most need this extra energy. It is extremely stressful to be meeting new people, learning new names, and, if you are new at your setting, finding your way around the building, the systems, and so on.

Towards the end of the first term, energy levels fall low, the nights become darker and the learners more fractious. Ask yourself – is the feeling that I can't cope a symptom of general tiredness? Will things seem better at the beginning of a new term, when I've had a holiday and I feel refreshed and ready to face my learners again? If this is the case, try to have a proper break from teaching during your holidays. Refuse to take any planning or marking home with you, book yourself a flight to somewhere sunny if you can afford it, and concentrate on recharging your batteries. That way you can plunge in with renewed vigour when you return to school the next term.

Overwork

It could be that you are tired because you are overworked – workload is a massive issue in the current education system. If you take on too much outside of lesson time, this can lead to problems dealing with your classroom teaching. You may have family or other caring commitments that cause you additional stress and leave you too exhausted to deal properly with handling the behaviour of your class.

Think very carefully about your extra curricular responsibilities. Although these activities offer a welcome change from classroom teaching, and a good opportunity to get to know your learners, they also mean that you have to stay late after a full working day. Your number-one priority has to be your health and sanity – learn to say 'no' to demands on your time when your stress levels are too high. Again, the term 'selfish altruism' applies here – be selfish enough to take care of yourself, so you're in the best possible state to help your learners learn.

The setting

On the other hand, it could be the school or college itself that is the problem: remember, your working environment has a powerful impact on behaviour in your classroom. Are your school buildings run down and uncared for? Is the ethos a negative and confrontational one? Is there poor retention of staff and a leadership team that does not support you properly? And is the behaviour policy ineffective in dealing with the issues that you face? If you have answered 'yes' to some or all of these questions, then it is likely that your setting is struggling to handle difficult behaviour.

If this is your situation, make sure you turn to other staff for support. If you feel that your personal situation is getting out of hand, and that you alone cannot even start to improve the situation at your school or college, then you will need to decide whether you are willing to stay. The most important thing is for you personally to stay healthy and happy – you won't be an effective teacher if you are unhappy or unwell.

Your personality

Different people react differently to different situations. Some teachers seem able to shrug off incidents of inappropriate behaviour, putting any problems behind them and moving quickly onwards. Other teachers take the same kind of incidents to heart, and find it almost impossible to forget about them. Many of us do get very emotionally involved with the job – it's almost inevitable when you are working with young people, some of whom lead very troubled lives. But if you are a sensitive person, you will need to find ways to cope with your emotional responses, particularly if you teach in a challenging school.

What are the danger signs?

A certain amount and type of stress is healthy: it is essential in keeping us energetic and 'alive', and keeps us from becoming dissatisfied with our work. After all, you probably came into teaching because you would have been bored by a typical office job. Teaching offers many different challenges, and it can be the most wonderful career in the world. On the other hand, a difficult teaching job can be too much for some people to manage, and there is no shame at all attached to feeling that you cannot cope.

Stress is a response to a difficult situation, and when we are stressed we produce high levels of adrenaline. Originally, the production of adrenaline helped us in a fight-or-flight situation, where our ancestors needed to be ready to flee from danger or to wrestle the proverbial mammoth to the ground. The problem in our modern world is that we can become overstressed, producing all this adrenaline without any means of using it up.

As a teacher, you have to stay and deal with stressful circumstances, rather than running away or resorting to physical solutions. If your school situation is problematic, and your stress levels are too high, your health could be put at risk and not even the most wonderful career in the world is worth that. The symptoms of stress vary according to the individual, but there are some common signs that you could look out for to check whether you are becoming excessively stressed by your work. If you have any concerns at all that your stress levels might be getting too high, visit your GP to ask for a proper medical assessment.

Physical symptoms

- **Difficulty sleeping:** if you are having difficulty sleeping, particularly on a Sunday night when you are preparing for the week ahead, you could well be experiencing high levels of work-related stress. Do you dream about your problem classes? And do your dreams become nightmares in which you can no longer cope?

- **Feeling sick:** that hollow feeling in the pit of the stomach is, I'm sure, something that many teachers, and certainly all those who have worked in a school where there are serious behaviour issues, can relate to. Do you feel sick when you are about to face your most difficult class, or classes? Or do you have that sick feeling all the time? If you do, you might be suffering from excessive stress.

- **Increased heart rate:** you might also find that your heart begins to beat faster because of the production of adrenaline. Does this happen to you when you are about to teach? Again, a raised heart rate can be a symptom of stress.

- **Sweaty palms:** if your palms become sweaty in tense classroom situations, this could be a further sign that you are over stressed.

Emotional symptoms

- **Loss of confidence:** when you feel that you can't cope with the behaviour of your learners, it is easy to lose confidence in your teaching abilities. Your perception of what is actually happening in your classroom can become distorted, and the problems you are experiencing might loom much larger than they are in reality.

- **Becoming defensive:** you might also find that you become overly defensive, expecting the worst from your learners. This can be counterproductive and can lead to a negative attitude towards your work and your learners.

- **Bursting into tears:** all too often, I have seen teachers (including myself) reduced to tears in the staffroom, or even in the classroom. What other job forces this sort of situation on its workers? If you find yourself feeling overly vulnerable and emotional, this is probably a sign of very high stress levels.

- **Becoming snappy:** when you or your colleagues are stressed, the temptation to snap at each other becomes greater, particularly if you are all dealing with similarly difficult learners. Again, poor relationships among the staff in a school can indicate a time of high stress, perhaps during an inspection or other stressful event.

How do you cope?

How, then, do you cope if your stress levels are high, and you feel that behaviour problems are getting on top of you? Firstly, follow the advice given in this book. Many of the tips that I give are simple to put in place, but will make a significant difference to behaviour in your classes. The strategies could take a while to work, so don't lose heart if they don't make an immediate difference. With persistence, you will start to make inroads into your problems. In the meantime, here are a few specific ideas for managing high stress levels.

Use your support systems

In my experience, the staff who work in schools are wonderful at supporting their colleagues. Use all the support systems that are available to you: an ECT mentor, a SENCO, a fellow teacher, a teaching assistant, plus friends and family too. Talk about your problems with someone sympathetic – sometimes all that is needed is a shoulder to cry on, or a caring ear in which to pour out your woes.

It can be very helpful to watch another teacher's classes – someone who you know has excellent classroom control. Although this option is usually only offered to newly qualified teachers, a supportive head might allow you to do some observations if you explain how helpful the opportunity would be. By watching how someone else copes with similar learners to your own, you will pick up some useful tips that you can utilise in your own classroom.

If you watch a teacher who has been at the school for a while, don't forget the power of a good reputation. If you are new to the school, you will still be building up your own positive word of mouth. Similarly, if you watch a member of staff who has a leadership post (head of department, head of year, deputy head), remember that this responsibility will also have an impact on how the learners behave for them.

Keep a perspective

In a difficult school it is sometimes hard to keep a perspective on what you are achieving. At primary level, you will be wholly or mainly responsible for teaching one class – no one else is having to cope with exactly this mix of children. At secondary and college level, a major problem is that you never get to see the learners in their other classes, and so you have no real idea of how they behave for their other teachers. Always remember, a poorly behaved class is not a reflection on your talents as a teacher, but a manifestation of many other contributing factors. Remember, too, that the world really is not going to end if your learners won't behave themselves. Try to avoid blowing up incidents of inappropriate behaviour into more than they really are. Bear this great quote in mind: 'Even in your worst lesson, nobody died.'

React from the head

Our instinctive reaction to rudeness or aggression is to take it to heart – we are human beings and not machines, after all. But every time teachers become emotional, this causes them stress and also shows the learners that they can 'win' by behaving inappropriately. Some learners love 'winding up' their teachers, and when we react emotionally, they have succeeded. On the other hand, maintaining a rational, intellectual response will show the learners that they cannot get at you. It will also help you think of ways to manage the situation in a calm and considered frame of mind.

Every time you feel your heart starting to race, and your emotions kicking in, take a moment to think about the situation from your head, rather than from your heart. Pause for a few seconds, or walk away for a moment, to cut the link between your emotional response and your actual reaction. Respond in a logical, thinking way, rather than in a sensitive, feeling way. Here are a couple of examples to illustrate the point.

For example...

The disruptive learner

Meredith is wandering around the room, disturbing the rest of the class and refusing to sit back down, despite being warned about possible consequences.

Your heart says: *'Why won't she do what I say? The rest of the class must think I've got no control over her. I feel so helpless. Now I'm getting angry. WHY WON'T YOU DO WHAT I SAY, MEREDITH?!'*

Your head says: *'Okay, this learner is refusing to do what I say, but it's not my fault; it's her own choice. Now, what am I going to do about it? Well, first of all I'll stay calm, that's important. Then I'll warn her, and if that doesn't work, I'll impose the consequences that I've told the class about'.*

The uncontrollable class

Your class is an extremely difficult one, and they are totally refusing to settle down and get on with their work. They are making loads of noise and throwing paper aeroplanes around the room.

Your heart says: *'Help!!! They're completely out of control! What am I going to do!? Someone might hear them and think that I can't control my classes. I'm never ever going to be able to get them settled down and teach them! Why on earth did I decide to become a teacher?'*

Your head says: *'Okay, things are going wrong here, but I'm not going to panic. First of all, it's not my fault; it's the learners who have decided to misbehave. Everyone says what a difficult class this is. I'll try to apply the consequences I've set, and if necessary I'll have to keep some of them in. I know, I'll go and sit with that table of learners who are waiting to start, thank them for being ready and see if that helps.'*

Take heart from small successes

When you are feeling really down, consider the small steps your learners have taken that might make you feel proud. For a teacher in a difficult school, or working with a difficult class, managing to get your learners to stay in their chairs may represent a huge achievement. Praise and reward yourself, as well as your learners, for these achievements. Teaching is a complex job, and there are many people who could not even start to make the progress you have made. Take a look at what your well-behaved learners are achieving as well: often, when we are dealing with generally inappropriate behaviour, it becomes easy to overlook the work and attitudes of the cooperative learners.

'The caring stops at five o'clock'

This line (given to me by a teacher who worked in a pupil referral unit) perfectly sums up the need to be able to cut off from the job, especially if you are a sensitive soul. It is inevitable that, to an extent, you will take the job home with you. But if you wish to stay in the profession for the long term, you must accept that you cannot change the world. You will probably come across children, teenagers, young people and adults whose lives outside of your setting are pretty miserable. Ensure that you raise any potential child protection issues with the designated safeguarding lead, but remember that your main role is as a teacher and not as a social worker. Do the best that you can during working hours, but leave school behind when you head home for the day.

Don't be a perfectionist

You simply can't be a perfectionist if you're a teacher – the job is far too complex and multifaceted to get it right all the time. When a lesson goes wrong, look for reasons by all means, but don't bog yourself down with excessive self-analysis. If a learner chooses to opt out of your subject, try your best, but don't stress yourself too much about it. As long as you are doing the best that you can for your learners, then you are doing your job. There is no point in dwelling on what is past and gone – keep learning, and always look to the future.

Take time out

There is no shame in sometimes making life easy for yourself, particularly if you are dealing with difficult learners on a daily basis. On occasions, give yourself a break, perhaps by showing a documentary, or booking your class into the computer suite.

Take time off

If you are suffering from high stress levels, go to visit your doctor. It could be that you are ill, and that you need to take some time off to recover. Similarly, when you have the flu, see that as a signal to have some time off sick, rather than muddling through until you can't go on any more. Do not feel embarrassed or ashamed if you need to take sick leave. Teaching is an extremely taxing profession, and you will not be able to work at your best if you are tense and stressed. Above all, make your own health your first priority.

A new career?

At some stage, you might have to ask yourself whether you are willing to cope any more with your school, or with teaching as a profession. This is a personal choice that only you can make, but one that you will obviously want to consider long and hard. It could be that you have become disillusioned with your current school, but that changing to a job somewhere else will refresh your outlook on teaching as a career. Only you can decide.

Whether you do decide to change jobs, or to change careers, I wish you all the best in your future. And please don't forget, teachers make a huge difference to the lives of all their learners. There are so many learners out there who need your talents and your help. And those learners who struggle with behaviour are in desperate need of your care and attention to help them succeed, no matter how much they might push you away. So, follow the advice in this book, keep plugging away, and I promise you that eventually you will be successful in 'getting your class to behave'!

Index

Teacher Toolkit

9781472910844

A compendium of strategies, ideas and advice, which aims to motivate, comfort, amuse and above all reduce your workload, by bestselling author Ross Morrison McGill, aka @TeacherToolkit.

Ross believes that becoming a teacher is one of the best decisions you will ever make, but after more than two decades in the classroom, he knows that it is not an easy journey!

He shares countless anecdotes from his own experience, from disastrous observations to marking in the broom cupboard, and offers a wealth of advice for all aspects of teaching practice, from lesson planning to marking and assessment, behaviour management and differentiation.

Complete with a bespoke Five Minute Plan in every chapter, photocopiable templates, QR codes, and more, Teacher Toolkit is a must read for newly qualified and early-career teachers.

Available to purchase now from www.bloomsbury.com/education

Follow us on X @BloomsburyEd and TikTok @BloomsburyEducation. Sign up to our newsletter for tips, previews and giveaways.

You Got This

9781801990196

You Got This! is the ultimate guide to succeeding as an early career teacher.

Whether you're searching for your first teaching job or preparing for your first parents' evening, this guide from experienced teacher and ECT mentor Andrew Taylor (aka Mr T, @MrTs_NQTs) is full of advice and support to show you the ropes and lend a hand.

The book covers all aspects of the Early Career Framework, including interview tips, preparing for statutory assessments, building positive relationships, managing workload and setting career goals.

With daily tips, coaching questions and case studies from ECTs, this book will ensure success from the very start and help you remember that no matter the hurdles, you got this!

Available to purchase now from www.bloomsbury.com/education

Follow us on X @BloomsburyEd and TikTok @BloomsburyEducation. Sign up to our newsletter for tips, previews and giveaways.

What Every Teacher
Needs to Know

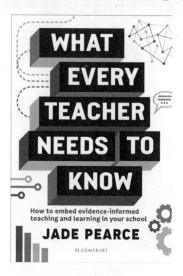

9781801990356

A concise, accessible guide for both primary and secondary teachers, this book distils key educational research into clear, precise guidance that can be used immediately.

Essential reading for research leads, heads of department, and teaching and learning leads, this book is ideal for any busy teacher or school leader looking to transform student outcomes through a research-informed approach.

What Every Teacher Needs to Know offers:

- summaries of 20 prominent research papers on effective teaching and learning
- key takeaways for classroom practice
- evidence-informed teaching and learning strategies
- examples across a variety of phases and subjects
- insightful case studies from practising teachers.

Available to purchase now from www.bloomsbury.com/education

Follow us on X @BloomsburyEd and TikTok @BloomsburyEducation. Sign up to our newsletter for tips, previews and giveaways.

The Ultimate Guide to Differentiation

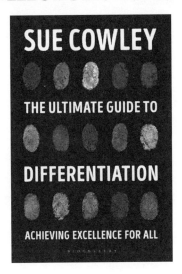

9781472948960

Over 90 practical and time-saving strategies for differentiation and adaptive teaching in every classroom.

Sue Cowley shows that we need to understand, acknowledge and celebrate the variety of approaches that teachers already use, as well as helping them to develop additional strategies. The book takes the reader through the different methods and approaches to differentiation and adaptive teaching, providing a step-by-step guide to each. It is broken down into five core areas - planning, resources, learners, teaching and assessment - which readers can easily dip in and out of.

Written in Sue's much loved honest and practical style, *The Ultimate Guide to Differentiation* will help teachers, practitioners and support staff feel confident that they are meeting the needs of every learner.

Available to purchase now from www.bloomsbury.com/education

Follow us on X @BloomsburyEd and TikTok @BloomsburyEducation. Sign up to our newsletter for tips, previews and giveaways.

How to Survive Your First Year in Teaching

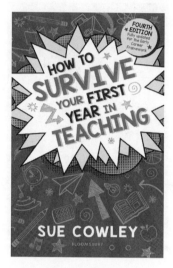

9781801991834

This new edition of Sue Cowley's bestselling book, fully updated for the Early Career Framework, is a must-read for all new teachers at the start of their career.

This introspective toolkit shows you how to not only survive but thrive during the first two years of your teaching career, and this latest edition provides practical new chapters on how to effectively manage your workload and gives plenty of useful teacher wellbeing tips.

Written in Sue Cowley's honest, accessible and down to earth style, this is an essential, practical guide to navigating your first two years in the classroom.

Available to purchase now from www.bloomsbury.com/education

Follow us on X @BloomsburyEd and TikTok @BloomsburyEducation. Sign up to our newsletter for tips, previews and giveaways.

Teaching for Realists

9781472985286

A funny and honest guide to surviving and thriving as an early career teacher, despite the challenges of the education system.

We all know the education system has its flaws, but they shouldn't stand in the way of providing the very best learning experiences for your pupils.

Omar Akbar offers a wealth of hard-won practical advice for avoiding frustration and developing teaching techniques that have a real impact in the classroom. Full of hilarious anecdotes and exploring hot topics such as pupil apathy, enriching the curriculum, Ofsted, data and behaviour, this book is a refreshing and uplifting take on what newly qualified teachers can do to have a happy, healthy and successful career in education – starting now.

Available to purchase now from www.bloomsbury.com/education

Follow us on X @BloomsburyEd and TikTok @BloomsburyEducation. Sign up to our newsletter for tips, previews and giveaways.